The Spiritual History of English

The Spiritual History of English

Andrew Thornton-Norris

British Library Cataloguing in Publication Data
A catalogue record of this book is available from the British Library

Printed and bound in the United Kingdom
Designed by Sarah@sarahbettsworthdesign.co.uk

ISBN: 978-1-904863-50-2

Social Affairs Unit
314–322 Regent Street
London W1B 5SA
www.socialaffairsunit.org.uk

To my Mother and Father

Contents

Preface

This book is the product of an intellectual, spiritual, and personal journey for which the model is that of St. Augustine of Hippo. I was brought up by lapsed protestant parents in England in the 1970's and 1980's. I had a normal English state school education and studied Philosophy, Politics and Economics at Oxford University (dropping the third subject after the first year.) My teachers were secular: liberals, socialists and even at Oxford, still, communists. I went behind the Iron Curtain whilst studying there to see what it was really like. After Oxford I wanted to write. It took me six years to discover that English Romantic literature was no longer possible. It had existed in the context of Protestantism. It took me another nine years to discover that this was no longer possible either. The logic that it had contained from the beginning had worked through to its conclusion: that Protestant orthodoxy was a paradox. I had become a classicist and an Anglo-Catholic, following T.S. Eliot; but now I found that I had no choice but to become a Roman Catholic. I had discovered that only the Magisterium could redeem the individualism of modern society. This is what the "Theology of the Body" of Pope John Paul II achieved: in revealing the harmony between the objective truth of Thomism and the subjective truth of modern philosophy and experience. This is an important moment in the history of Western civilization and I write in honour of that fact. I would like to thank the people who helped me to write this book.

Introduction

This book is about the relationship between religion and literature in England. It is also a book about the language and its spirit. It examines the incarnation of metaphysics or belief in the language and the literature of a people. It begins with the foundation of England at the time of the Anglo-Saxon invasions and it follows this relationship through to the present day, when the prevailing religion or belief-system is secular or pagan: a religion of humanity, of human rights, equality and material progress, enforced by law. As Edward Norman has shown, this 'modern state is as confessional as its predecessors', it's just that the underlying belief-system it enforces is not quite so easy to identify.[1] This book is in part therefore a response to the author's experience of this secular state, its system of education and its secular culture.

It considers the spiritual response to those formative experiences of someone seeking the truth of human existence. Which may seem to be a rather quaint activity in the secular materialist marketplace, where the struggle to realize one's self in the world, to achieve one's potential in materialist terms, is the norm. Nonetheless, it considers the various possibilities available to someone seeking a way of understanding and articulating the experience of being in the world, and the taking leave of it, which is most satisfactory. It is an attempt to understand and to assess the dominant culture in which people are raised and educated: what it has to offer to the individual, and to humanity as a whole, both now and in historical terms. The attempt is therefore an intellectual one, an investigation of literature, philosophy, theology and history, among other things.

But it may be that a conclusion can only be reached through a *transcendence* of the intellect. While such an understanding will have an intellectual and rational basis, the origins and consequences of that process are emotional or instinctive, and defined by experience, including cultural experience. The conversion of the heart is more important than that of the mind, for that is what governs the will, while the consolation and hope provided are directed to the heart not to the intellect. This may be challenging to the post-enlightenment rationalist mentality but that mind has recently begun to examine the basis of its own faith in pure reason. And it is a similar idea to that of the unconscious motivation for actions: one of the ideas that has disrupted Enlightenment confidence in pure reason, the other being the absence of a reliable deity.

The relationship between these different aspects of the human personality includes the relationship between individual and collective knowledge, the authority of inherited tradition and the cultural development of individual consciousness, creativity, and judgement. Any conclusion drawn will be based on a judgement of the perceived truth of the evidence as presented and experienced, and of the character and nature of the witnesses, rather than simply the validity of scientific or philosophical argument. Belief is formed by more than rational argument: metaphysics and belief are related but not identical matters. Belief provides the context for the discussion of metaphysics, and for judgements about it, but metaphysics does not determine belief: it is its consequence. Metaphysics may help to understand, structure and account for belief, but belief operates at a deeper psychological level: the level of experience, the level at which literature and culture operate.

The subject matter they deal with, their content, is that of experience, which includes religious experience and that of contemporary secular humanism or paganism. The dominant manifestation of this is the Puritan-derived belief that spiritual goodness ('election') on a social or a personal level is manifested in material circumstances, achievement and progress, in health, wealth or technological advance, for example. The answers provided by this secular humanism did not address certain aspects of the author's own experience; in particular, those *in extremis*, of difficulty or blessing. The adequacy of sending someone out into the world with the spiritual resources of modern secular humanism was therefore, at the very least, questionable. The secular explanations, responses or accounts did not have the language, understanding or reasons with which to respond to, express or account for such experience. Whether it was seen from an Anglo- or Roman Catholic perspective, the only real alternative to secular humanism or paganism was the same: orthodox ecclesiastical Christianity.

It is unlikely that any spiritual tradition outside the Western ecclesiastical one, or other materialist ones, could have been satisfactory. Even in the post-Christian West, the historical construction of culture and the personality is such that any growth or development of spiritual under-standing is in practice and ultimately inseparable from Christianity and its cultural legacy, while the maintenance of orthodoxy is likewise inseparable from the authority of a church. Movement in any other direction is, in this respect, simply a form of Protestantism. Meanwhile socialist materialism offered no real spiritual alternative to a capitalist one. Each are 'world-immanent' rather than 'world-transcendent' means of interpreting and giving meaning, purpose and depth to existence.[2] Materialism is the problem not the solution. Although intimations of this prospect had been gleaned from some of the historical literature encountered through the secular education and culture, and literature itself had provided some answers, it only went so far, and could not answer all the questions.

In seeking a secular explanation and knowledge in literature, poetry was a possibility, and the most prominent contemporary poet of the time was Philip Larkin. His master was Thomas Hardy, and the tradition they represented was one derived from Puritanism. This was the 'English Line' of Romantic poets, whose origins were in Milton, Gray, Collins and Wordsworth, and ended with Edward Thomas,

Robert Frost, and Larkin himself.[3] This remains the dominant English poetic sensibility or mode of response, even in such technically 'modernist' writers as Ted Hughes and Geoffrey Hill. It is the literary incarnation of the empiricist attitude to the natural world contained within the rise of modern science, and the sceptical philosophy, Puritanism and romanticism that are associated with it. It is a modern form of paganism: manifested variously as a cult of the individual personality, the mind, the body, creativity, pleasure, nature or other political, material or cultural values. It includes a mystical understanding of nature, the world or the person which believes in things beyond those verifiable through scientific method, while rejecting the dogmas of ecclesiastical Christianity.

And it includes Scientism: which is the widespread belief that nothing may be believed in which is not verifiable through scientific method, or is not susceptible to scientific proof. This represents an attitude to the scientific method, and so to knowledge, which is one of pure faith. The assumption that the scientific method is the only reliable or valid method of answering all questions, in any field of human knowledge other than the physical, is not in itself provable or verifiable as true, and is thus self-defeating.[4] The grounds for faith in religion or the arts as reliable or verifiable means of acquiring knowledge in these fields have, by comparison, secure foundations. They are the means by which humanity has always sought to understand itself, its existence, its nature and its moral universe, and it has brought immense rewards. The alternative has failed to do so.

In one respect therefore this work is an *Apologia Pro Vita Sua*, a history of religious opinions or beliefs and their relationship with literary tendencies. In a more important sense, however, this book is a lament: that there is no living literary tradition or that it is so prosaic as to consist of nothing more than non-fiction. It is sometimes argued that non-fiction has become the only literary form capable of dealing with the complexity of the present. This may be grounded in the pre-modern tradition of literature as rhetoric. The ancient world made no value distinction between poetic or prose literature and so perhaps neither should we. In examining these claims this work is also a plea, or a manifesto, for the revival of literature in England. It argues that the revival of orthodox ecclesiastical Christianity may be the precondition for this revival, as our historic literary tradition depends upon it in ways to be examined.[5] It is, therefore, also a consideration of the possibility of and conditions necessary for poetry and poetic prose, or fiction, in the present.

The work of Maurice Cowling provides the escape from the dominant romantic sensibility, in particular through his study of the intellectual process of de-Christianization, *Religion and Public Doctrine in Modern England.* The process is that of the conversion of the confessional state from one founded on Christianity to one founded on secular humanism or paganism. He asserts that it is 'Catholic, ecclesiastical Christianity... which *is* Christianity',[6] that, despite the importance of other forms, it is the Church which has provided that essential continuity over centuries which Christianity has enjoyed. He implies that it is unlikely that the Anglican form can survive in a secularized society, that an 'independent ecclesiastical power' is required, as well as that the clergy have the 'requisite normality, serenity and self-confidence to address the Christianity which is latent in English life'.[7]

What Cowling saw was that all political positions were derived from religious positions, as were artistic or cultural tendencies. Cowling's question when attempting to understand any thinker, writer or political actor was always 'What is his religion?' Any attempt at reduction or translation of these religious motivations or beliefs into secular or ideological terms would always leave out something essential. It is thus a liberation from the ideology of the post-Christian consensus, which shapes contemporary education and cultural activity.[8] The idea is then to project this approach back to the relationship between religion and literature beyond modern England, and also beyond doctrine, to look at the wider manner in which religion is incarnate in artistic values: the subject which obsessed T. S. Eliot throughout his life. Cowling considered literature to be a crucial modern vehicle of doctrine, both religious and post-religious.

He began his first volume with a quotation from Carlyle's Lecture on 'The Hero as Man of Letters' of 1840: 'The writers of Newspapers, Pamphlets, Poems, Books, these are the effective working church of a modern country.'[9] The third volume began with another line from the same work, 'Of all Priesthoods, Aristocracies, Governing Classes at present extant in the world, there is no class comparable to the Priesthood of the Writers of Books.'[10] And he concluded with the question of whether there was really a connection between Christianity and any cultural and academic endeavour. Whether a Roman Catholic could find Catholicism in a particular style of architecture, for example: as Pugin had done in the Gothic, identifying the Classical with paganism; and as Pevsner was accused of doing in finding in 'international modernism' a post-Christian religion of 'egalitarian uniformity'.[11]

This book is an examination of those texts and of the English soul, but it is also a book about religion and culture in general, and the effects modernity has had on each, which are similar across cultures. Modernity itself is examined by studying a particular version of it: England and its literature – a version of modernity quite benign by comparison with some others. But spiritual questions and those of culture and civilization are always serious, as are those of the relations between religion, politics and culture. England, as the first industrial nation and the earliest example of a nation state, with a long literary culture to sustain it, is a good laboratory in which to examine it. As an account of national and literary development into the modern world it is exemplary.

It is also a book about the English language, about the

values and influences that have gone into its development. As the spiritual history of literature as it has developed in England, it also includes discussion of works in Latin, Greek, French, Spanish and Italian, and works in English produced by writers who were born or lived in other countries. The language developed in a particular place, among a particular group of people, subject to particular influences. So the language incarnates some of the characteristics and experiences of these people, as does the literature. This is the spiritual history of a literature, but also of a language and a people who speak it. And as that language has spread, so those influences, that literature and that culture have spread, right across the world.

While this book is a history of English literature from the introduction of the tongue to the present day, it is not an encyclopaedic history, but rather an attempt to understand the present by examining the past. It recognizes that the orthodoxies surrounding the study and practice of literature, and of religion, are in dire need of revision. It is of the essence: short rather than extensive. Its subject is a specific element of the history of literature: the metaphysics of literature, and the manner, method and mode of its incarnation in literary form. It deals with the metaphysical and formal essence of that history, rather than the detail. It spends more time in dealing with poetry than with prose, because that is the most spiritual literary art: the closest to music and to prayer.

It does so also because the nature of the spiritual transformation can be seen most clearly in the development of the poetic image and of technique. Clarity, breadth, limpidity and simplicity are spiritual as well as rhetorical virtues, and the spiritual poverty of language is of the highest spiritual significance. The widespread use of jargon and code in academic and intellectual presentations of intellectual, cultural and spiritual matters is a deliberate impairment of communication, a refusal to be intelligible. It is a practical rejection of the possibility of a common criticism and judgement, and a disdain for truth itself. 'We have sunk to a depth in which re-statement of the obvious is the first duty of intelligent men', wrote Orwell.[12]

It has become possible, customary, conventional even to view the history of English literature from a non-Christian perspective, although its history is inseparable from that religion. The distortion of this perspective, which Eliot described as a 'new kind of provincialism not of space, but of time',[13] is a barrier to the real appreciation and under-standing of English literature, and the Christian and Latin Classical foundations of the European civilization and culture of which it is, or was, a part. It is also a barrier to realizing the personal significance and value of liturgy, prayer and religious traditions, our spiritual inheritance and understanding, and the culture it engendered for almost two millennia.

The metaphysics and the culture that have replaced it leave the individual alone to face his difficulties and blessings, and the profound questions of mortality, sin and loss that are always with us. The fruit of this is the existential sickness of the art and culture we see around us. And also, vice versa, this decline in cultural standards has affected the liturgy of the Church. The tolerance of inferior texts is a consequence of the decline both of cultural standards and orthodox belief. The coarsening of liturgy is a coarsening of the spirit as well as of the sensibility. The Word of God has been made incarnate in English, both through the translation of Scripture and the development of the vernacular liturgy. So, the language has been at times a religious language akin to Arabic, Latin, Hindi or Hebrew.

In England the peculiar doctrinal confusion of its Erastian reformation has meant that continuity of liturgy has been more important than that of doctrine, and so contemporary liturgical destruction is of particular significance. The work of translation from Latin, Greek and Hebrew, and from the modern European vernaculars, is a living proof of the importance of interpretation, of the active engagement with texts, rather than the naive and sometimes dangerous belief that their meaning is literal, immanent and indisputable. It shows the religious need for a culture which sustains the critical faculties of humanism, to ensure that religion is a living intellectual as well as practical belief, to ensure that it does not become a superstition or too literal in its interpretation of sacred texts, but also to ensure that humanism does not become a religion in itself.[14]

The crisis facing Christianity in England affects it what-ever ecclesiastical form it takes, as it affects religion, wisdom, understanding and belief in general. But the different church and religious structures are affected in different ways, and some doctrinal and liturgical responses are more successful than others. Throughout history the relationships between English literature, the Church and the Crown have been intimate, so, the challenges to sacramental worship in our day, whether in the Roman or the English church, bear upon the fate of each. It may be, however, that only a belated counter-reformation in England led by the monarchy can resolve that crisis, with all the implications for English culture that that implies. What we identify is a religious problem, for which logic dictates a religious solution.

It might seem strange to associate literature with the Church, especially when so much of it seems designed to provoke, challenge or reject the Church. But this shows the power, influence and authority that the Church has had within the culture, without which that culture is weakened if not destroyed. At the centre of the study therefore is the relationship between literature and belief, and the central question is whether literature requires a particular religious context to survive: whether for English Literature this context has been and can only be ecclesiastical Christianity. Without such a context, literature may become a merely private activity, unsustained by any sense of collective purpose at the deepest level, and therefore divorced from the collective memory and any possibility of collective achievement, all of which are essential for the great work of art.

The liberal belief-system that has taken the place of Christianity is just the opposite of such a religion. It is a refusal to believe in anything, except the freedom to believe in and to do whatever you want, so long as you allow others to do the same. The resulting relativism and multi-culturalism is corrosive of tradition, especially literary tradition. Despite the fact that 'Englishness is the principle of diversity itself... '[15] it still requires the preservation of a historic core for diversity not to become dispersion. Meanwhile that liberal belief-system shows itself as relative, deconstructing itself so to speak. When belief becomes a purely private matter, faith is no longer disciplined or deepened by religious authority or doctrine. And the orthodox Christian believes that the doctrine of Original Sin, and the life in the spirit which is the result, is the greatest liberation of all.

A Christian literature may be, as Cowling suggested, 'the only plausible link between historic orthodoxy and any orthodoxy which is likely to command the future'.[16] What the Church did, as we shall see, was to sustain a culture of preservation of the standards of the past against which the achievements of the present could be measured. It thus established and sustained a living tradition, within which creativity could be nourished and guided. It also provided a context within which art or the individual were prevented from becoming a religion themselves. The intention therefore is to show another way of looking at English history, and English cultural history in particular, to dissolve the boundaries of understanding between religion and culture and politics, and to uncover the hidden or hermetic theology, which is perhaps even more important in a post-Christian culture.

1. Edward Norman, *Anglican Difficulties*, pp. 70–1.
2. Distinction 'world-immanent' and 'world-transcendent' in Michael Burleigh, *Earthly Powers*, p. 5, derived from Eric Voegelin in his *The Political Religions*. The Hegelian idea of the State is one in which religious attributes are found in the secular state, and is the origin of the genocidal state.
3. In *The English Line*, John Powell-Ward associates this tradition with Puritanism.
4. See Amos Funkenstein, *Theology and the Scientific Imagination*, for the lifting of the Aristotelian proscription of metabasis, the translation of methods from one science to another, and John Milbank, *Theology and Social Theory*, for the modern invention of the secular not as temporal (between the Fall and the Last Things) but as a spatial, a place beyond the sacred. See also Benedict XVI, *Faith, Reason and the University*, for the need to 'overcome the self-imposed limitation of reason to the empirically falsifiable, and... once more disclose its vast horizons'.
5. George Steiner, in *Real Presences*, gives an account of the reason why belief in God may be essential to the Western creative tradition. He sees the origin of creativity as being a 'pious envy' or rage, a determination to create an alternative universe which is more to the author's own taste. In this way all great art contains the real presence of the original creator as well as that of the immediate creator, and it is why the postmodern world with its belief in absence lacks such art.
6. Maurice Cowling, *Religion and Public Doctrine*, vol. 3, pp, 697–8.
7. Ibid., p. x.
8. Ibid., pp. xx–xxiii.
9. Thomas Carlyle, 'The Hero as Man of Letters', 19 May 1840, in *On Heroes and Hero-Worship*, cited Cowling, *Religion and Public Doctrine*, vol. 1, p. xi.
10. Cited Cowling, *Religion and Public Doctrine*, vol. 3, p. 3.
11. Questions posed by David Watkin, the architectural critic. Cowling, *Religion and Public Doctrine*, vol. 3, p. 693.
12. George Orwell, review of Bertrand Russell, *Power: A New Social Analysis* (January 1939), *The Collected Essays, Journalism and Letters of George Orwell*, pp. 375–6.
13. Eliot, 'What Is a Classic?', *Selected Prose*, p. 130.
14. See T. S. Eliot, 'Religion without Humanism'.
15. Peter Ackroyd, *Albion*, p. 448.
16. Cowling, Religion and Public Doctrine, vol. 3, p. 698.

Chapter 1

Religion and Literature

I write under the light of two eternal truths—Religion and Monarchy; two necessities, as they are shown to be by contemporary events, towards which every writer of sound sense ought to try to guide the country back.

(Honoré de Balzac, Author's 'Introduction' to
The Human Comedy [1842])

Literature is perhaps the most intellectual of all the arts. Its material is the very medium of thought itself, while the visual and performing arts act upon the senses and subsequently stimulate reflection. It is ironic therefore that in no other art than poetry have the English so excelled (and thereby avoided embarrassment alongside their European neighbours, whose achievements in the other arts are so superior) when they are supposed to be an un-intellectual and pragmatic people. However, the times are not auspicious. Since Milton and Puritanism, and what Eliot described as 'the dissociation of the sensibility' from the intellect, English poetry has been the primarily the 'poetry of the unpoetic' (the phrase is from J. S. Mill). It has incarnated a melancholy absence: of the real presence of the divine in the everyday, which was the Medieval English experience, and is that of Catholic cultures today.[1]

Furthermore, in the post-war period there has been a decline in the quality and achievement of English literature, especially poetry, by comparison with the achievement of the previous several hundred years. The relationship between religion and literature has escaped attention in recent times because each has receded from its former place at the forefront of the culture and because these recessions are related. In his 1948 *Notes towards the Definition of Culture*, T. S. Eliot described the 'culture of a people as an *incarnation* of its religion', adding that this way of looking at culture is 'so difficult that I am not sure I grasp it myself except in flashes, or that I comprehend all its implications'.[2] While modern people might like to believe that they can do without Christianity this does not mean that religion can be so easily avoided, although it may be that literature can.

In 1927, at the time of his conversion to Anglicanism and naturalization as a British subject, in a *Criterion* review of Bertrand Russell's *Why I Am Not a Christian*, T. S. Eliot argued that 'one ceases to be Christian only by becoming something else definite – a Buddhist, a Mohammedan, a Brahmin'.[3] The recession from Christianity has not resulted in a mass of such conversions, let alone Russell's, merely the attenuation of Christianity into a variety of sub-cults that coalesce around a simple premise: that belief in the Christian religion is either outdated or irrelevant, with little or no agreement as to why or what should take its place. From Eliot's perspective this is merely an extreme form of Protestantism and the variety of doctrines that have taken the place of orthodox Christianity are more or less explicit versions of lapsed Christianity.

Genuine atheism or actual conversion are equally rare, and a generalized agnosticism or superstition is the consequence of a determination not to think about religion. The attempt of these secular or godless religions to ignore religion and concentrate on making the best of this world has not, however, resulted in the successful transcendence of belief in the supernatural. Rather it has enabled the relaxation of the spiritual discipline theology provides as a bulwark against superstition. Belief in human progress or perfectibility may for instance depend on faith in the ability of technology to liberate us from human history or to alter human nature. Meanwhile, the plethora of beliefs and doctrines that has succeeded Christianity constitutes the disagreement that lies at the heart of its civic aspect, Liberalism, and the democratic system it implies. Without that disagreement there would be no need for the religious impartiality that liberalism proposes, and which becomes a doctrinal attack on religious belief per se: the pursuit of political freedom becoming a veil for relativism.

It may also be that modern politics have made the existence of a literary high culture impossible, consisting as they do in the rejection of all authority beyond that of the 'will of the people'. This undermines the standards necessary to establish literary excellence as popularity becomes the chief criterion of literary success. This is the political incarnation of modern religion and a common feature of the recession of Christianity and Literature. Its literary incarnation is predicated on the denial of authority external to the individual, in matters artistic as well as spiritual or political. While the artistic culture is created by and for people whose sole external political or spiritual authority is the negative one of democratic liberalism, no artistic authority is acknowledged beyond that of individual taste. The attempt to establish any sort of hierarchy being elitist, racist, patriarchal, or otherwise an affront to the dignity of free-thinking or feeling individuals.

Furthermore for many the pursuit of art has itself become a form of religion whereby the individual explores, uncovers and is thereby united or reunited with his own true self, whether in creation or consumption (note the similarity with some redemptive political creeds). Art becomes a form of autonomous spiritual exploration that is incompatible with the religious order that existed prior to the modern period; and with orthodox Christianity per se, where religion is a separate and prior activity, with prior moral claims. It is rather a religion of art, a religious belief in writing and the self-becoming of the individual writer or artist, its significance for society and its status as a moral end in itself. This romantic idea of art is also that each man should decide for himself what he likes, as much as what he should believe, and that any attempt to impose or cultivate standards is an infringement of his dignity.

This culture achieved its clearest incarnation in

Romanticism, which had its ostensible origins in the eighteenth century, but was observed in embryo during the Renaissance, and has never left us. Its early stages of development were largely a fruition of what had gone before, albeit with a new element, Renaissance Humanism. This revival of Classical Humanism, which went on to triumph at the Civil War, when it was made fully incarnate in literature by Cowley and Milton. Their Elizabethan and Jacobean antecedents had been formed by the combination of the old and new cultures. Their particular achievement, as well as the Book of Common Prayer and the Authorised Version, were perhaps a consequence of the fine balance between the two. Carlyle described it as 'the outcome and flowerage of all that had preceded it... attributable to the Catholicism of the Middle Ages'.[4]

Romanticism proper was partly a literary reaction to the Enlightenment, but it was also associated with the revival of interest in, and new archaeological and other knowledge of, ancient Greece. This was convenient for its political associations with democracy and republicanism, radicalism and individualism, liberty and equality, all of which were in turn, a reaction to the remaining legacy of Roman Imperialism from the Middle Ages. It was accompanied by a revival of interest in and regard for literature in the vernacular, including Anglo-Saxon and Celtic literature, or what sometimes passed for it.[5] It came with a preference for the Elizabethans and Jacobeans over the English Augustans, and an acknowledgement of the spiritual paternity of Milton. It was thus a further rejection of the Latin cultural tradition that had been associated with ecclesiastical Christianity for over a thousand years.

Southey described it in 1807 as being a school 'half-Greek half-Gothic', and it was equally corrosive of the Latin Classical tradition. Even Eliot did not reject some of its criticisms of Johnson, who in his Late Renaissance Latinity had believed that modern English poetry began with Cowley and Milton, themselves Latinists. Indeed Eliot in his poetry self-consciously fell foul of Johnson's criticism of the Metaphysical's use of 'heterogeneous images yoked by violence together' and 'thoughts, so far fetched as to be not only unexpected but unnatural'.[6] In doing so he set out to rediscover the essence of the Metaphysical Poetry that he considered to be so 'highly civilized' and relevant to the complex society of his day. It revealed the relationship between philosophical beliefs, feeling and behaviour, and so provided a way of testing those beliefs.

He developed a view of Metaphysical poetry with its zenith at the time of Dante, when the mind and the emotions were fused in a sensibility that saw the 'senses thinking' or 'sensuous thought',[7] such that Dante could offer 'the most comprehensive and the most ordered presentation of emotion that has ever been made',[8] partly as a consequence of the order and comprehensiveness of Thomist, or Catholic, theology and philosophy. The ongoing 'disintegration of the intellect' meant that this supremely 'metaphysical' moment was to be repeated, but to a much lesser degree of perfection in the schools of Donne and of Baudelaire.

It was said that the problem with espousing 'classicism' in the twentieth century, perhaps even in the eighteenth, was that while 'the 'romantic' mood is always with us, as an impulse to break down accepted conventions, the 'classical' requires a settled and self-confident society with widely shared assumptions to sustain it' and it thus 'amounted to nothing more than another version of romantic nostalgia'.[9] Eliot accepted some of this in his essay on Baudelaire, saying that, 'a poet in a romantic age cannot be a "classical" poet except in tendency'.[10] But he also viewed the distinction as one, 'between the complete and the fragmentary, the adult and the immature, the orderly and the chaotic',[11] which depended on the willingness to accept external authority in aesthetic, moral, social, political and spiritual life: a distinction essentially between Protestantism and Catholicism, Orthodoxy and Heterodoxy.

Romanticism is by contrast a sanctification of the

imagination, akin to the sanctification of other faculties such as reason or empathy, which would be impossible to the orthodox believer, despite his recognition of the power of art to communicate his own message. This sanctification for Eliot was part of the 'disintegration of the intellect', part of the 'dissociation of sensibility' from the intellect.[12] This was the abandonment of intellectual and spiritual engagement for the pure pursuit of self and sensation through creation, the rendering helpless of criticism through the rejection of external standards beyond apparent authenticity and power of expression. There was thus a clear downward path from the Italian poetry of the thirteenth century, and that of Chaucer in England just after. And this was related to the decline in the intellectual background from the integration of the personal and the philosophical that was achieved in the Middle Ages.

From another perspective Ted Hughes, Poet Laureate and anthropologist, in 1993 described the metrical aspects of this history. The challenge to orthodox metre from unorthodox, the challenge to quantitative, classical or continental metre from native, alliterative forms was related to the struggle between the English Church and 'what it would call Paganism resurgent'.[13] This 'had been the dominant theme of European poetry ever since' Shakespeare. While Chaucer 'was the sensitive underside of the [Norman] courtiers', whose 'innovation was to naturalise in an English poetry the up-to-this-point alien culture of the Court class'.[14] This was one of his last critical forays; in his first in 1962, in the last years of Eliot's life, he had himself addressed 'Context'. Speaking of the relationship between the French Revolution and the English Romantics, the apparent unrelatedness of the poetry of Wordsworth, Coleridge and Blake to the 'important issues', 'social and political' of the day and the later obviousness of that connection in spirit, Hughes remembered that 'strange observation' whereby 'Damon, quoted by Plato, says that the modes of music are nowhere altered without changes in the most important laws of the state'.[15]

Formal qualities of works of art and their subject matter are thus related to the broader values and beliefs that they incarnate. The most profound criticism is that which elucidates this relationship between belief (and their practical or political incarnation, for example, in morality and laws) and literature. It may be a direct or indirect relationship, the latter occurring, according to Eliot, in metaphysical poetry when 'you have a philosophy exerting its influence, not directly through belief, but indirectly through feeling and behaviour'.[16] Our subject is the spiritual history of English, in particular, but this approach may be applied elsewhere, and indeed to the other arts. This relationship between religion and literature, and this spiritual history therefore, has two aspects: one metaphysical and one formal.

The first is the religion or belief held by the writer or period, or contained within the work, whether conscious or unconscious, and the second is its incarnation in literary form. As 'the Word was made Flesh and dwelt among us' so a metaphysic or belief is incarnate in literary form. It is an approach to literature, religion and culture which understands them as intertwined, as different aspects of the same thing. It sees the beliefs, actions and modes of behaviour that go to make up a way of life as united in a way that is clearest in traditional cultures or the ancient world, where religion and culture were regarded as one and the same thing and were denoted by the same word. It is akin to the anthropological approach, although it avoids the secular pieties and prejudices of that academic discipline.

Should it be established that there have been such declines in literature and Christianity, it is possible that each is the consequence of related or unrelated external causes, perhaps technological, social or political change, and that each decline is therefore unrelated or only incidentally related to the other. It is argued here, however, that whatever a writer writes, and whatever a reader reads, is intimately related to what they believe, as is everything else that they do. As Ted Hughes puts it: 'How things are between man and his idea of the Divinity determines everything in his life, the quality and connectedness of every feeling and thought, and the meaning of every action.'[17] Any examination of literature is therefore illuminated by attention given to this spiritual aspect. While others may wish to give priority to the technological, social and political aspects of this history, we shall concentrate on the religious.

It is possible to see the relationship between religion and literature as one of mutual exclusion, of incompatibility. Religion has often been inclined to see literature, creativity and the arts as threatening to or distracting from faith. This is seen in the ban upon representation in Islam and Judaism, in the Puritan closure of the theatres, the Protestant attack on images and ritual, and Catholic hesitancy about replacing plainsong with polyphony, in case it was too sensual for a sacred setting, or even the use of guitars. At the same time, a vital literature, an open and enquiring intellectual culture, has been seen as impossible when the intellectual darkness of revealed religion is too strong. This is what lies behind the imagery of the Dark Ages, the Renaissance and the Enlightenment.

As Sicco Polenton, the earliest Renaissance historian of Latin Literature, put it, poetry and eloquence slept between Juvenal and Dante. Although he didn't say that this was because of Christianity, the implication of much Renaissance and later humanist criticism is just that. And V. S. Naipaul, perhaps the greatest living writer of English, repeats it today, talking of long ages without literature, including 'the long Christian night'.[18] Naipaul has been influenced in this judgement by his experience of Islamic countries and of Latin America, which share the experience of an imperial revealed religion, indeed one which was transmitted from Islam to Catholic Spain.[19] However, he says of literature in Europe today that it has been squeezed out by 'too much television'.[20] And this reflects a wider world which combines 'high technological advance and very low intellectual development'.[21]

One aspect of the decline in English literature, which may impair perceptions of it, is the obscuring of domestic tradition by vitality from abroad: of which Naipaul is a part. This derives in particular from the spheres of past English influence or control, including the Commonwealth, Ireland and America, but also from almost the whole of the rest of the world, by virtue of linguistic and cultural expansion. The question is whether this is an assimilation of other traditions into the English, as occurred before with classical and continental literature, or rather the emergence of a variety of hybrid, mongrel or ghetto literary cultures, which incorporate elements of immigrant experience of England on the one hand with colonial and post-colonial experience on the other.

It is thus the question of the extent to which Geoffrey Hill, Ted Hughes, R. S. Thomas, Harold Pinter, Tom Stoppard, V. S. Naipaul and Salman Rushdie for instance inhabit a central English tradition. To what extent the presence in their work of international and non-European elements is a departure or derivation from that tradition, a non-English literature replacing an English one, so to speak. To what extent it is the development of a literature and a post-Christian theology of the English-Speaking Peoples, based on modern communications technologies, as well as prior imperial history, and including India, the Caribbean and North America. How this has challenged, reinforced or diluted traditional English ideas of themselves and whether it represents or heralds a renaissance of English culture, as happened with previous European assimilations, or an annihilation of it.

If this broadening of literary tradition in English disguises the fact that England no longer has a literature of its own, with the standards of quality and achievement that it used to have, then the identification of those standards is essential. This is not just the question of whether an international modernism conflicts *With the Grain* of an *English Line*, as argued in two books with those titles on the subject.[22] But it is also the deeper question of the underlying nature of that English tradition, its roots, sources, essential and superficial elements: the question addressed by Peter Ackroyd in his book, *Albion*. He argues that the culture has always been expansive, acquisitive and assimilative, while retaining an essential Christian and antiquarian or classical core.[23] The question now is whether that essential core can survive the recession of Christianity, whether England is still capable of producing a culture and a literature comparable with that of its past, and what the religious component of such a revitalized culture might be.

The pragmatic solution may be a challenge to the individualist and thus, in the end, relativist values that originated at the Reformation. The chief political phenomenon related to these developments is democracy, which implies an egalitarianism and relativism regarding standards. These democratic or individual rights cultures tend to undermine established or inherited cultures, including inherited classical and Christian values, by undermining their authority, and replacing them with the modern individualist values and commodities of the market. The question is how any standards or authority external to the individual can be upheld when a philosophy and a practice prevails that makes the sole source of those standards or authority the individual conscience. This is also the problem of the role of individual conscience and external authority in religion, the problem of justification by grace or works, the question of transubstantiation and the nature of the sacraments.

It is a problem of theology but also the problem of the institutional survival, and therefore the survival at all, of religion. This is the problem that has faced religion and hence culture since its institutional triumph at the Reformation, since the beginning of the emergence of modernity. In religion it determines the nature of ecclesiastical organization and social and moral teaching. In culture it is the similar question of the authority of the tradition, or the historic community, over the individual personality, where respect for tradition includes respect for accumulated wisdom. This book traces this relationship through the earlier period, when a literature was sustained by a collective faith that was orthodox or continuous with the historic faith. That was, in other words, external to the individual.

It is therefore a study of the overall spiritual decline of a people whose most exalted achievements in literature and religion may be over. Which raises the underlying question of whether material prosperity such as we now enjoy is possible without spiritual and cultural poverty. Whether an advanced technological and prosperous society with considerable personal freedom and political stability can also be a society that enjoys artistic achievement comparable with what went before, and a healthy spiritual life. Even some communist countries have maintained a high tradition of the performance of classical music and literary education, for instance: but what we are concerned with is original creation. It is the question of whether mass democracy, with the attendant danger of the cultural and spiritual tyranny of the majority, is compatible with these higher achievements and values.

The nature of causation between political change such as this, social change such as industrialization and the breakdown of the old order and religious and cultural change is not straightforward. What matters is that this religious change has taken place and that it has been accompanied by cultural decline. That this may be a consequence of the rise of the middle classes attendant upon industrialization and economic growth is not the question. Rather it is whether this change constitutes progress in anything but a raw material sense, whether it is possible to achieve this material and technological advance without spiritual and cultural decay. With widespread material wealth such as has never been seen before, or enjoyed by such a broad group of people, at least in developed countries: is spiritual and cultural poverty inevitable, or a passing and contingent phase? Is the necessary consequence of industrialization an egalitarianism or relativism regarding values, and if not, how can it be avoided? Is a democratic view of art desirable, and if not how can it be made compatible with a society founded on such a basis?

It is also the question, addressed by V. S. Naipaul, of how this decline in English literature bodes well or ill for those other cultures, where the influences that have been brought to bear in England may now take effect. It is obvious that so-called Anglo-Saxon or Western cultural and economic imperialism may bring material benefits, and sometimes political benefits through the promotion of liberal political practices. But this must always be weighed against the effect on the cultural and religious changes that we shall see develop in Britain, as the first industrial nation. This resulted in the literary consequences that we describe, and the religious problem that is faced by England, in common with many developed and developing nations. The decline of traditional societies often poses challenges to religious and cultural aspects of those societies. The problems we describe in England have taken more violent forms in other places.

Modern politics are preoccupied with material wealth, its production, distribution and the procurement by it of social goods such as health, education and security, as well as private goods. However the idea of freedom of this modern liberal religion is opposed to the orthodox Christian idea of freedom, which was central to the English identity and political tradition from the very beginning. In it true freedom is freedom from sin, and Christ is the liberator from sin. In consequence, the activity of the state is limited to the realm of the body, rather than the soul. This derives from Christ's teaching in Matthew 22.21, 'Render therefore unto Ceasar the things which are Caesar's; and unto God the things which are God's.' Thus the church becomes the religious authority to which ethical questions are referred, beyond the realm of the state.

For Benedict XVI, Augustine's *De Civitas Dei* is an attack on this political religion, the 'divinisation of the polis', which 'rates the State's good higher than the truth' in which 'behind the unreal Gods of civil religion stands the only too real power of the demons'.[24] As the state reclaims this realm, in political ideology or in Islam for instance, so the Western idea of freedom is compromised: in Pope Benedict's phrase 'where there is no dualism, there is totalitarianism'.[25] It was the problem that lay behind the confessional state in England from Elizabeth until 1829, and especially after 1688. As the Elizabethan Martyr Edmund Campion said at his trial; 'I will willingly pay Her Majesty what is hers, yet I must pay to God what is his.'[26] The front cover image of this book, taken from the Hinton St Mary Mosaic, discovered in Dorset in the 1960s, illustrates the point. The form of the image is thought to have been taken from that of an emperor on a Roman coin, but in fact represents the earliest known image of Christ in Britain.

This pagan intrusion of the state into the soul has been revived in modern times, in England, America and the European Union, as much as in Germany or Russia. In democratic countries this is manifested as a 'dictatorship of relativism which does not recognize anything as for certain and which has as its highest goal one's own ego and one's own desires'.[27] Benedict's predecessor identifies the origin of this phenomenon, whose political consequences they both lived through, in the philosophical foundations of modern thought. After Descartes, God was no longer prior, as the foundation of all being, including human being, upon which everything depended. The result was that Good and Evil became subjective, and the radical Evil of the twentieth century became possible. This is the result of what John Paul II describes as 'the decline of Thomistic realism'.[28]

Ludwig Wittgenstein revealed Descartes's arguments to be logically as well as epistemologically flawed. How could he have begun, for instance, with the proposition 'I think, therefore I am' without a language with which to formulate such a proposition ? Language requires a community to exist, so he could not possibly ground his epistemology in the thoughts and the words in which they appeared in his own mind. There are also problems with the basic assumptions about the self or reason itself which he makes. Wittgenstein's deconstruction of the Cartesian subject in his *Philosophical Investigations* is part of his challenge to Scientism and 'a determination to insist on the integrity and the autonomy of non-scientific forms of understanding'.[29]

We shall see how this process was made manifest in literature. And that is the conclusion of this book, and the conclusion of our literature. Our literature is dead: it died with our faith, and its culture of tradition and continuity. With it the foundations of judgement and discrimination, the foundations of the idea of literature as the art of writing and the foundations of belief have all been undermined. But with it also died the anti-Catholicism which went alongside the patriotic Protestantism that was the creation of the English Reformation and the origin of that relativism: now may be the time for that to change. It may not have been possible to tell this story of English literature until now when it is all but over in this mode, and so can be seen as a whole. If it is over, then that may be because Christianity was essential to it, and a way has not yet been found for literature to survive without it.

---

1. See Powell-Ward, *English Line*. The poet Roy Campbell believed that English people travelled to continental Catholic countries as much to escape the restricting atmosphere of their (post-) protestant society and culture as for the weather.
2. Eliot, *Notes towards the Definition of Culture*, p. 30.
3. Eliot, *Varieties of Metaphysical Poetry*, p. 100, n. 15.
4. Carlyle, 'The Hero as Poet', *On Heroes and Hero-Worship*.
5. As in the poems of 'Ossian', a forged attempt to create an independent Celtic literary identity, and the medieval forgeries of Thomas Chatterton – see J. C. D. Clark, *Samuel Johnson*, pp. 77–87, for former. The attempt was taken up with more success by Sir Walter Scott.

6. Samuel Johnson, *The Lives of the Most Eminent English Poets, With Critical Observations on their Works*, vol. 1 'The Life Of Cowley' (1779), paras 56 and 71.

7. Eliot, 'Swinburne as Critic', *The Sacred Wood*, www.bartleby. com/200/.

8. Eliot, 'Dante', *The Sacred Wood*, www.bartleby.com/200/.

9. Baldick, *Criticism and Literary* Theory, p. 74.

10. Eliot, 'Baudelaire', *Selected Prose*, p. 233.

11. Eliot, 'The Function of Criticism', *Selected Prose*, p. 70.

12. Eliot, *Varieties of Metaphysical Poetry*, pp. 223, 227; 'The Metaphysical Poets', *Selected Prose*, p. 64.

13. Ted Hughes, 'The Snake in the Oak', *Winter Pollen*, p. 375.

14. Hughes, 'Myths, Metres, Rhythms', *Winter Pollen*, p. 367.

15. Hughes, 'Context', *Winter Pollen*, p. 32. Benjamin Jowett's translation is 'when modes of music change, the fundamental laws of the State always change with them' (Plato, *The Dialogues of Plato*). Neither specify the direction or mechanism of causation.

16. Eliot, *Varieties of Metapysical Poetry*, p. 295.

17. Hughes, 'The Great Theme: Notes on Shakespeare', *Winter Pollen*, p. 109.

18. Interview, *Financial Times* (21 August 2004).

19. See V. S. Naipaul, *Among the Believers*, p. 126. But he will admit that 'even the rigidities of a revealed faith, a feeling for the spiritual might prompt wonder, and science and the search for knowledge would have begun' (Naipaul, *Beyond Belief*, p. 208).

20. Interview, *Financial Times* (21 August 2004).

21. *The Nation* (Thailand) (11 April 2004).

22. Donald Davie, *With the Grain*; and Powell-Ward, *English Line*.

23. '[The] history of the English imagination is the history of adaptation and assimilation' (Ackroyd, *Albion*, p. 448). The 'conflation' or mixing of forms in English writing which is the consequence, of biography, history and the novel for instance, describes Ackroyd's own work. The classical rhetoric which governed European literature, including poetry, fiction, history and biography, until the eighteenth century, likewise saw all forms as equal.

24. Aidan Nichols, *Thought of Benedict XVI*, p. 143.

25. Nichols, *Thought*, pp. 259–60. This dualism is the same as the 'philosophical diffidence' that V. S. Naipaul extols in American and Western society in his lecture 'Our Universal Civilization' to the Manhattan Institute (30 October 1990). He contrasts it with the 'shriek' of 'philosophical hysteria' found elsewhere, a metaphor he takes from Joseph Conrad.

26. Edward Norman, *Roman Catholicism*, p. 28.

27. Joseph Ratzinger, 'Homily at the Mass for the Election of the Roman Pontiff' (18 April 2005).

28. John Paul II, *Memory and Identity*, p. 13.

29. Ray Monk, *How to Read Wittgenstein*. Also see John Milbank, Catherine Pickstock and Graham Ward (eds), *Radical Orthodoxy*, Chapter 3.

Chapter 2

The Ecclesiastical History of English

We begin then with the story of the ecclesiastical origins of English literature, the establishment of the Latin Classical tradition, the first part of the spiritual history of the English people and of their language, which is spoken now throughout the world. Before the 'Middle Ages', the island of Britain was inhabited by people we describe as ancient Britons, or sometimes as Celts. The majority of these people were in fact here long before the arrival of the Celts from Central Europe, a few hundred years before the Romans. These were people of different races, the majority of whom had been in Britain, and elsewhere in Europe, especially Northern Spain, throughout the long period of pre-history. After the Celts, the Romans came, and saw, and conquered; and then left again. The Romans themselves changed between the time that they left Britain and the time that they returned five hundred years later, in the person of St Augustine of Canterbury, sent by Pope Gregory the Great. They had eschewed their paganism, but not the culture that they had built up around it.

The history of English, of the English people, the English Church, the English language, and of English literature begins with Gregory the Great's mission: in the lifetime of the Prophet Mohammad, and so on the cusp of the ancient and modern worlds.[1] It was Gregory who first described as 'Angles' the pagan Germanic peoples who had come to Britain; to whom he sent his mission two hundred years after the pagan Romans had left. These barbarian invaders consisted of many different Germanic races, including Saxons and Jutes, but they only became known as the 'English' because that was how Pope Gregory described them. He is the only Latin speaker on the continent at the time known to have done so, and he was said to have done so because he wanted to make them 'not Angles but angels'.[2]

Englishness was not and would not become an identity with a simple racial basis, nor indeed were British, Roman or Celtic identities.[3] It was defined by the pope: the ex-pagan Germanic-speaking invaders were distinguished from the Britons by the specific papal mission to them. It was they who became the adherents of the Church of the English founded by St Augustine at Canterbury. It was they whose story was told in the first masterpiece of the literature, though not of the language. It was written in Latin, the international language of learning and liturgy, and it was appropriate that it was so, for the English were quick to respond to Gregory's mission and to renounce their barbarian past in favour of Latin religion and culture.

The Venerable Bede's *Ecclesiastical History of the English People* begins with the story of the Britons, and their fate, after they had been brought Roman and Christian civilization, and proved unworthy of it. That history, Bede tells us, he got from Gildas, 'their own historian'. Bede then tells how, upon arrival in their promised land, God transferred his favour to the English; with a warning to avoid the mistakes that the Britons had made if they wanted to avoid their fate: subjugation. '[T]he English were God's new "chosen" nation elected to replace the sin-stained Briton in the promised land of Britain.[4] Bede's model for this story was the Old Testament, the history of the relationship between God and his original Chosen People, Israel.

He had spent almost his entire life studying it at Wearmouth and Jarrow, so he knew very well its underlying theme: if his Chosen People obeyed him, God would bless them; but if they disobeyed, he would punish them. Responding to Gregory's initiative, Bede made this the underlying plot of his *Ecclesiastical History*. From then on it was to become the underlying plot of their actual story: a religious plot with the Church at the centre.[5] And it was told in a literature which included the writing of history, which in England has been regarded as primarily a form of literature rather than of scholarship.[6] England understood itself therefore from the very beginning as a nation with a providential relationship with God, and therefore with a special relationship with the original People of the Book. As Ted Hughes suggests, this was to lead in our own times to the restoration of the state of Israel itself.[7]

This understanding of themselves as an 'elect' nation recurs throughout English history and literature, but what was God's purpose for them? This is the fundamental question for a Chosen People. It underlies the ongoing dialogue within the nation and its literature regarding its identity and its relationship with other peoples. And it reveals the assumption that underlies the continued existence and vitality of the English state, its language and its literature, for longer than any other. This vitality was revealed when, following the Norman conquest, the invaders adopted the language of the conquered: just as had happened in the collapsing Roman Empire. As Patrick Wormald identifies, this is because English had already, like Latin, become 'a language of literature and government'. So there is a direct connection between the fact that England is 'the world's oldest continually functioning state, and that English is now its most widely spoken language'.[8]

The simple answer was that they were to obey God's Law as revealed in the Old Testament and modified by the New. King Alfred began his lawbook with a translation of the Law given to Moses in the book of Exodus, and a description of how this had been changed by Christianity.[9] Thus the English tradition of liberty began with liberation from sin. The other answer is provided by God himself, in the form of outcomes: as punishments or rewards for various actions, by Providence, and this answer is revealed in the study and interpretation of history. This is the job of the Church, but it is also the job of writers, and of a literature that includes histories. As Edward Norman puts it, 'the whole point about the history of Israel is that it was the *education* of a people'.[10] And education is best when it is written.

Thus the sense was born that the English were a Chosen People, with a special mission to civilize their neighbours, wherever in the world they might be. It was fathered by Pope Gregory, articulated by the Venerable Bede and embodied in the Church which St Augustine founded. And it therefore predated the Reformation by about a millennium. This sense of a special mission to civilize has followed the language and its speakers wherever they have gone, although the idea of that civilization has come to be understood in different and more materialistic ways, that would be unrecognizable to Bede, Alfred and many other English historians.[11] It is this changing conception of the nature of their civilization that underlies the spiritual history of English literature, and the people whose language and literature it is. It is this record that shows how that prophetic or providential question has been answered. How their history has been interpreted, understood and directed in a prophetic or providential manner: the stories that they have told and the examples that they have taken for themselves.

But this interpretation and understanding may provide different answers at different times to different people. And it is not only the job of the Church: for they must also be responded to and implemented by secular rulers and leaders, who command the assent of the governed. While the history of the Church and works of ecclesiastical literature such as theology and preaching reveal one side of the understanding, the other side is provided by the practical realization of this understanding in wider culture. This in its highest cultural form is literature, and its most practical form is that of government, both at home and abroad. The continual English note is one of pragmatism, whether of government or writing, rather than the continental tendency towards the abstract.[12]

The history of the development of the answers provided to this question comes from both religious and other sources. The Israelites had their prophets, priests and kings, their Law and their communal record in a series of books, the Old Testament of the Bible, and especially the Torah; and so have the English. They have their Bible, their Church history and works of theology and liturgy; but they also have their literature, which also reveals their religious understanding and their language as sanctified. The 'providential question' is answered therefore not just in policy or in law, in church practice or communal life, but in the creation of a culture: the incarnation of the religion of a people, a revelation of their belief. For the English, it reveals their understanding of themselves as a Chosen People, their understanding of the nature of their God and their relationship with him.

Bede provided the first answer to the 'providential question', which we may describe as the orthodox answer: it was that spiritual order lay in adherence to the Roman Church and to the classical culture in which the Christian faith had been incarnated. The Romans, when they became Christian, were not quite sure what to do with the great culture that had been built up alongside the pagan religions of Greece and Rome. After much debate, the definitive answer was given by St Augustine of Hippo in his *City of God*: his epitaph on pagan Rome after the fifth-century Sack, attributed by many to the replacement of classical paganism by Christianity. His answer was that 'whatever was good, true or beautiful could be used in the service of the gospel' proceeding, as it must, from the divine goodness. The Church thus determined to incorporate that great culture into its very being. Christianity was as inseparable from the Classical world into which it was born, and in whose tongue its Testament was written, as it was from its Jewish flesh and blood. The historical timing of Christ's birth was decisive.

The incarnation of classical paganism and humanism in classical culture was consummated by the incarnation of the Christian religion in the common Latin Classical culture of Medieval Europe. While doubts remained about the moral value of much of that literature, it was impossible to deny it as a model of literary and intellectual excellence, and as an educational example. Its philosophical ideas became integrated into Christian theology, providing it with the intellectual resources to elucidate basic concepts such as the Trinity. There was a Greek Renaissance which saw rhetoric as the embodiment of Greek intellectual values. The 'cult language and the literary language of Christianity' was Greek until Latin took over.[13] By the sixth century rhetoric was the firm basis of its literary and educational understanding and practice. The Dark Ages saw the retreat of this culture into the monastic cell, where it remained until Charlemagne brought it back into common life.[14]

It was this Latin Classical culture therefore which, after Gregory's mission and Bede's *Ecclesiastical History*, became the incarnation of the religion of the English. It was identified with the Church of the English at Canterbury, while the other 'Celtic' tradition continued to develop independently. Less than ten years before Bede was born the two parties had met at the Synod of Whitby in 664, and debated the date of Easter. Despite the fact that the monasteries of Northumberland were dominated by Irish monks, and the rest of the country was still over-whelmingly 'Celtic', the Roman party prevailed, confirming the commitment of the English which Bede grew up to articulate. The English understood themselves as a Chosen People whose ideal of civilization was that of Rome and the universal Church, with its Latin Classical culture. This was before Charlemagne and six hundred years before Dante. They retained and developed a distinct culture and way of doing things, as did the French, Spanish and Italians. But all those individual cultures were from the outset inseparable from the common European civilization of the 'Middle Ages'.[15]

This Latin Classical culture had another essential element, its emphasis on tradition rather than the individual as the source of intellectual authority.[16] This is the essence of the Latin Classical tradition, of the 'transmissional techniques of grammar, rhetoric, the "liberal arts", the schools'.[17] These were the means by which classical literature and learning was transmitted to the Latin Middle Ages, and hence into the European vernaculars; a process led by Cassiodorus in Calabria and Isodore of Seville. It was not until the eighteenth century that the concept of the creative imagination was born.[18] Chaucer shared this reticence and he showed that the essence of the English sensibility was assimilation or reinvention not creation.[19] This was associated with a distinctive 'antiquarianism' which became an obsession with history, tradition and the past as the source of intellectual and cultural authority and identity. It came from Bede and the Latin Classical tradition, and it has not left us. In this sense England is no less Catholic than it ever was.[20]

If Bede's was the orthodox answer to the providential question, we can see what a heterodox answer, or answers, might be. The centre was Rome, and the papacy, as the spiritual successor to the Roman Empire and its Classical culture. The conversion of Constantine and his removal of the Roman Imperium to Constantinople left the way clear in Rome for the papacy. The periphery and the resistance to it comes from those who wish to assert their autonomy, whether in political, spiritual, artistic, intellectual, moral or other spheres. In other words, to deny that classical and Christian culture its universality, its catholicity. There are two tendencies, pushing or pulling in two different directions, one centrifugal and one centripetal. If Rome was the centre of one type of spiritual and intellectual authority then the resistance to it could come from many directions.

But it is at bottom a single tendency: away from this centre of authority towards the dispersed, decentred authority of the individual person or the individual group: away from historic or classical or ecclesiastical authority towards the authority of the individual, the present or the future. This is the defining note of modernity, when the ongoing attempt to resist orthodoxy has had its greatest successes. The rejection of English membership of the universal Church led first to

Protestantism and then to the rejection of Christianity itself. But that orthodoxy still exists and like King Arthur may yet return.

That legendary king had Celtic origins, and stood for the opposite, anti-Roman or insular tendency in English and European life: the Romance or vernacular literature and the remnants of non-Roman paganism. Barbarians were how the Romans and the Greeks described those who lived outside their borders, and they included the Celtic, British and Germanic peoples.[21] It is significant that the origins of later Protestant theology were in eastern Germany and Switzer-land, the latter with strong Celtic roots. In Britain, the borders of the Roman Empire had been with Scotland and Wales, hence the identification of this resistance with the 'Celtic'.

In the disagreement with those who wished to remain part of the Universal Church, with its Latin Classical culture, those who wished to resist it might identify themselves with the 'Celtic', 'British' or anti-Roman cause, but they were not always identical with it. Charlemagne would transform this opposition on the continent by establishing a Holy Roman Empire which included barbarian Germans, and made Paris the centre of its intellectual culture. The foundations were thus laid for the emergence of French vernacular literature, and therefore for Middle English. Both would be Latin and Classical, but the English would achieve a balance between the two tendencies. Or rather it would transcend the difference, as it had already begun to do by incorporating both within the Anglo-Saxon Latin Classical culture.[22] It was this culture that Charlemagne reintroduced into post-Roman Europe, after the Moors had disrupted the Mediterranean power structure of the original Roman Empire, and brought the ancient world to an end.

The present is one in which this balance, between tradition and creation, education and innovation, external and internal authority, has been lost. Bede defines for us the nature of the incarnation of metaphysics in English literature.

He shows us our self-understanding as providential and Augustinian: England as Anglo-Saxon but an essential part of the Latin Classical culture that succeeded the conversion of the Roman Empire. And he shows us it in the literary form of an Ecclesiastical History, written in Latin. The history of English literary form begins with alliterative verse, brought over by the Germanic speakers who became known as the 'English'.

What we now know as English poetry is both alliterative, or accentual, and syllabic: its music has always been a counterpoint of these two elements. The latter element was introduced from Latin continental Europe, especially France and Italy. Later, elements of Classical poetic form or prosody were added to this, thus extending the accentual-syllabic repertoire. Thus the two metaphysical elements of English culture, the Germanic, Celtic or Barbarian and the Latin, are incarnated in literary form. Some, such as Coleridge, Hopkins and Ted Hughes, have argued that the development of these two elements was between an authentic, native or people's poetry, and an alien, or elite poetry. It is possible then to see the alliterative tradition as native, 'English', 'British' or 'Celtic', while the Latin Classical forms are continental and, therefore, alien.[23]

However, as we have seen, the Anglo-Saxon forms, were the poetic forms of the English people and their language, who were at the time a central element of the Latin Classical culture. Baptized in England by Pope Gregory, confirmed at the Synod of Whitby, and embodied in the Church at Canterbury as the Church of the English, they were an integral part of the universal Church with its Latin Classical culture. In fact, the development of the vernacular in every European country accompanied the gradual disintegration of the unified Latin culture that was the heritage of the Roman Empire. This was begun by Germanic incursions, and completed by the Islamic break-up of the Roman dominance of the Mediterranean, which 'threw Carolingian culture back to agricultural level'. Germanic culture was assimilative, the Arab was not .[24]

This was the origin of feudalism, but also of the transference of the Latin Classical culture into the vernacular. The medieval was as marked as the modern period by periodic renaissance, the rebirth of classical and humanistic learning and reacquaintance with the common sources of European culture. The Celtic and Anglo-Saxon culture was the first of these, the Carolingian the second, and the twelfth-century saw the third. While the Latin Classical culture was transposed into Romance forms of the vernacular on the continent, in England the same culture was transmitted into a Germanic vernacular, with a Germanic rhythm and melody, and hence verse forms. It was in the monasteries of England and Ireland that classical culture, in the form of manuscript copying, was preserved, as barbarism and destruction ravaged the rest of Europe.

While the English would keep their own tongue, write alliterative verse, use a distinct 'insular' method of writing their manuscripts, and develop distinct ecclesiastical and spiritual traditions, their culture was as inseparable from the Latin Classical culture of Europe as the Romance cultures. Although *Beowulf* represented the underlying inherited and persistent culture of the Anglo-Saxon aristocracy, their conversion was to a church whose culture was that of the Latin Classical tradition, and they were committed to it. Indeed the personnel of the Church and the Anglo-Saxon aristocracy were interchangeable, as they were across Britain, Ireland and indeed Europe, at the time.[25] The Church remained the locus of literacy throughout this period and *Beowulf* was the exception in the literate culture of the Church and the monasteries.

As the Romanesque architecture of the Normans was prefigured by the Latinate style of the Anglo-Saxons, of which much less remains, the introduction of French and Italian forms by Chaucer was an equivalent development of pre-existing English poetic form. The poetry of a new 'middle' English language was not an introduction from an alien culture: their culture was as continental as the pope who had invented it and the Holy Roman Empire which had adopted it. It was the other inhabitants of Britain who were different, 'barbarian'. Chaucer confirms the English membership of this common culture, which was not therefore an 'up-to-this-point alien culture' at all, as Ted Hughes describes it. He underestimates the depth and durability of this underlying sense of identity, which was *proved* by the fact that the Anglo-Saxon idea of England and its language survived the Norman Conquest and Viking invasions, despite the complete change in the personnel of the ruling class. This sense of identity and tradition was to persist.[26]

While the spread of literary forms among the different tongues of a common culture may have been to spread novelty and innovation, from Latinate to Germanic, it was in no way the intrusion of an alien element. What were alien were the limited traditions that persisted outside the Anglo-Saxon part of this part of the new Roman Empire, and to which Hughes's characterization might thus apply. The poetic form that became English poetry was the assimilation of traditions within a common Latin Classical culture. While there may have been a distinction between the culture of the court and the culture of the people, there is no reason to suppose that the latter was in any way more authentic than the courtly culture of the Anglo-Saxons which was itself Latin and Classical.

What Hughes articulates is an interpretation which has been dominant in England since the Romantic movement, but whose origins lie far back. It is to find in a so-called native tradition something essential that is missing in the classical, in orthodoxy.[27] However the prosodic orthodoxy that Hughes identifies is the prosodic orthodoxy of the continental syllabic tradition that was introduced during the reign of Elizabeth. He identifies this with the rise of the spirit of Puritanism and hence rationalism, and the demise of both the pagan and the Catholic traditions which preceded it. Thus Hughes's conception of individuality and subjectivity is a very different one from the modern rational liberal or romantic version. Tradition and authority are a liberation from individuality and subjectivity, in politics as much as religion and art.

The metaphysics of ecclesiastical Christianity was incarnated in a literary form, the Latin Classical tradition, that included both accentual and syllabic verse forms. There was also a dissenting tradition, associated with rejection of the Latin Classical tradition, but without a real presence in a formal literature. The Romance and Anglo-Saxon types of medieval literature were contained within a Latin Classical culture, which, although they might tend towards a more vernacular, Romance, or 'romantic' culture, were still the product of an educated and orthodox elite. Dissent and neo-paganism would not reveal itself until the theological explosion of the Reformation, which did not have genuine forerunners, in its rejection of ecclesiastical Christianity.[28]

The medieval period was marked by periodic renaissance and the development of vernacular literature, but it was also marked by intellectual or metaphysical orthodoxy. The Latin Classical tradition was thus always 'classical', and it was only the coming to temporal power of theological dissent which enabled a formal literature that was 'romantic', individualistic or a cult of individual creative personality to emerge. T. S. Eliot described this process as 'The Disintegration of the Intellect', and he saw it clearest in poetry. That collapse was completed in the process Ted Hughes saw underlying Shakespeare's lifetime, albeit pacified during Elizabeth's reign; and which was articulated as the underlying plot of all his mature works: the Puritan Cultural Revolution.[29] While conventional literary history describes this period as the birth of English literature, for us it is an ending.

The idea of a Chosen People is of dubious orthodoxy if it is identified with a nation-state, as it was to be in the Erastian English Reformation. Before that it was identified with the

Church of the English, which was also a part of the universal Church. It was, as Augustine put it against the Donatists, part of the *ecclesia omnium gentium*, the Church of all peoples.[30] It is thus the Church which is the successor of Israel as the 'People of God', not the nation. This deepens the sense in which the English were identified with the Latin Classical tradition rather than barbarism: for they were identified as a nation from the start with their church, by the pope. It also suggests therefore that the redefinition was a separation not just from a particular spiritual conception of themselves but from an entire cultural tradition, and their own identity.

It is ironic therefore that that redefinition was associated with the introduction of new continental verse and dramatic forms. This was no 'autonomous vernacular', as romantic literary history claims, for the paganism of the classical authors was the staple of the medieval liberal education. English literature began in Latin, the Anglo-Saxon culture enabled Charlemagne to lay the foundations for the emergence of French as the first vernacular literature. In Provence the Celtic and Germanic traditions of the North met those of the Latin South. Italian emerged from the influence of the troubadours in Provence, which Dante later transformed, from its Albeginsian heretical form into othodoxy. Dante's was the greatest achievement of any literature, and a crucial inspiration, alongside Boccacio, for Chaucer, and his reinvention of the Latin Classical tradition in Middle English.

---

1. Ernst R. Curtius, *European Literature*, p. 21, argues that the division between the ancient and the modern worlds is the rise of Islam.
2. Patrick Wormald, 'Bede, the *Bretwaldas* and the origins of the *Gens Anglorum*'; also *Ackroyd*, Albion, p. xx: 'The notion of Englishness itself was a religious one from the moment Pope Gregory sent Augustine to England with the mission of establishing a Church of the English in the light of his celebrated if apocryphal remark *"non Angli sed angeli"*.'
3. Nor were German, French, Spanish or Italian, after the Goths, Franks and Lombards had taken over.
4. S. B Greenfield and D. G. Calder, *A New Critical History of Old*

English Literature, p. 58, cited by Ackroyd, *Albion*, p. xx.

5. See articles by Wormald in the bibliography and J. C. D. Clark, *Our Shadowed Present*, Chapter 2, for the mechanics of this becoming the underlying plot, fiction becoming fact.

6. Ackroyd, *Albion*, p. 255.

7. Ted Hughes, *Shakespeare and the Goddess of Complete Being*, p. 519.

8. Patrick Wormald, 'Anglo-Saxon Society and Its Literature', p. 19.

9. Patrick Wormald, 'Enga Lond'.

10. Edward Norman, *Anglican Difficulties*, p. 114.

11. Ackroyd, *Albion*, p. 28: a 'religious view of history prevailed until the end of the seventeenth century, while nineteenth-century historians such as Acton and Macauley employed the secular religion of Whiggism to fashion their narratives'.

12. The twelfth century was typical: '[t]here is no English Aquinas, whose scholasticism rose into the Empyrean, but rather John of Salisbury whose books were concerned with the art of government' (Ackroyd, *Albion*, p. 129).

13. Curtius, *European Literature*, p. 68.

14. Curtius, *European Literature*, p. 75.

15. Ackroyd, *Albion*, pp. 32–4.

16. Ackroyd, *Albion*, p. 126.

17. Curtius, *European Literature*, pp. 394–5.

18. The ancients 'did not know the concept of the creative imagination. They had no word for it. What the poet produced was a fabrication... poetry was mimesis, "imitation" and indeed "imitation of men doing something"' (Curtius, *European Literature*, pp. 397–8).

19. Ackroyd, *Albion*, pp. 152–3.

20. Ackroyd, *Albion*, p. 126.

21. From the Greek for 'foreign', *barbaros*.

22. Ackroyd, *Albion*, p. 36: 'the Celtic and the Classical – are somehow amalgamated and thereby enlarged within a common sensibility'. Also Curtius, *European Literature*, p. 35: 'English national characteristics and forms of life are neither Romance nor Germanic – they are English.' And 'England is a "Latin" country, and we ought not to have to go to France for our Latinity' (Eliot, *Criterion* [October 1923], p. 104).

23. Hughes, 'Postscript to Myths, Metres, Rhythms', *Winter Pollen*, pp. 366–72, 366–9; Hopkins described it as 'Sprung Rhythm' (*Poems and Prose*, p. 188).

24. Curtius, *European Literature*, pp. 24–5.

25. Partrick Wormald, 'Bede, "Beowulf" and the Conversion of the Anglo-Saxon Aristocracy'. As Simon Schama puts it, 'the Church in Anglo-Saxon England (just as in Ireland and Pictish-Scotland) was a natural extension of the aristocracy' (*History of Britain*, vol. 1, p. 52).

26. Wormald, 'Enga Lond', p. 18.

27. Ted Hughes, 'The Snake in the Oak', introductory note, in *Winter Pollen*, pp. 374–5.

28. Curtius, *European Literature*, p. 108: 'And yet even the pagan [goddess] Natura never entirely vanishes from consciousness. Even in the tenth century she is occasionally referred to and called by her Greek name.'

29. Ted Hughes, 'The Great Theme: Notes on Shakespeare', *Winter Pollen*, p. 118.

30. Nichols, *Thought*, pp. 41–5.

Chapter 3

The Disintegration of the Intellect

The process by which the Latin Classical culture developed between the fifth and the twelfth century and its decisive influence on the emergence of vernacular literature is described in detail by Ernst Robert Curtius in *European Literature and the Latin Middle Ages*. He wrote the book in internal exile under the Nazi regime as a form of protest against it, an attempt at the deepest level to understand and explain how things had gone so badly wrong. 'What we are dealing with is literature – that is, the great intellectual and spiritual tradition of Western culture as given form in language.'[1]

The vernacular was derived from the reforms of Charlemagne, led by the Anglo-Saxon Alcuin, building on the Latin Classical tradition that developed in England in the seventh and eighth centuries. It had been passed to them by Cassiodorus in Calabria, Isodore in Seville, and, after them, the Irish monasteries. The result was that French was the first vernacular, emerging in the twelfth century, which had implications for English which was dominated by it from the Norman Conquest to Chaucer. The vernacular was a result of the confluence of national or local characteristics and the transmission of the Latin Classical tradition. The apotheosis and subsequent collapse of that Latin Classical culture into modernity is described by T. S. Eliot in his account of *The Varieties of Metaphysical Poetry* and elsewhere. Central to both accounts is Dante.

Curtius cites Goethe '"Dante appears great to us, but he had a culture of centuries behind him" while Carlyle heard in him the voice of "ten silent centuries"'.[2] This reminds us of Sicco Polenton but also that the Latin Classical culture was sustained during this time by the Church. Without the Church there would be no classical antiquity, we would have no knowledge of it.[3] In order to understand the development of the Latin Classical culture in England, and the period from Bede to Chaucer in particular, we examined continental developments. We remained within a common European and Catholic culture: the roots of the vernacular were Latin, Classical, ecclesiastical and English. The fruit of the Latin Middle Ages was the twelfth-century renaissance and Dante. The fruit of the Middle Ages as a whole was the literature of the 'Renaissance', including English literature from Chaucer to Johnson.

For Eliot, Dante was the greatest of metaphysical poets, and among the greatest of all poets. Chaucer was not, in Eliot's account, a metaphysical poet, but one who describes the world as it is. He was the 'greatest of English poets who came so soon after' Dante, in whom 'the human spirit reached a greater sum of range, intensity and completeness of emotion than it has ever attained before or since'.[4] They were the first self-conscious authors of a vernacular literature in their respective tongues to rival Classical literature. This signalled an end to the Latin Middle Ages. We shall conclude our study with a comparison of two contemporary writers in the 'Latin' and Anglo-Saxon traditions. The former were primarily poets while our contemporaries write prose: the earlier derives from oral traditions, whereas the latter assumes literacy.[5]

Eliot's account of Dante is important for us for what it allows him to go on to say about English poetry. Metaphysical poetry in England was confined to the life of the first Charles, from Donne to Cowley. It was to return in France, however, in the nineteenth century, in the school of Baudelaire, 'a man of distinctly metaphysical mind'.[6] It was this school that was Eliot's, and therefore Modernism's inspiration. Pound said of Eliot that, 'he has trained himself *and* modernized himself *on his own*'.[7] But he had not: he had taken foreign and ancient masters. Metaphysical poetry is not therefore a large part of the history of English literature, but it reveals the intellectual background of literature, a specific manner in which metaphysics is made incarnate in literature, and how a poet makes use of and transforms his material.

The difference between Dante and Chaucer is that they add to our experience in the two different ways that it is possible for poets so to do. 'One is by perceiving and recording accurately the world – of both sense and feeling – at any given moment; the other by extending the frontiers of the world.'[8] According to Eliot, metaphysical poetry occurs when an intellectual statement or subject, such as a philosophical or theological idea, is translated into images which enable those ideas or concepts to be 'seen' and 'felt' rather than thought, 'so that the world of sense is actually enlarged'.[9] He describes three metaphysical moments in poetry: in Italy in the thirteenth century, England in the seventeenth, and France in the nineteenth. 'Implicitly, there was a fourth moment at hand – Eliot in London in the twentieth century.'[10] He compares Dante and Donne, and their schools, and shows the deterioration in the quality of the Metaphysical image that takes place between them.

This deterioration was the consequence of deterioration in the intellectual background of these poets. The harmony of the Middle Ages, reaching its zenith in Aquinas, was replaced by the intellectual turmoil of the reformation and counter-reformation. This deterioration takes a major step forward in Descartes, with his inauguration of modern philosophy. In poetry ideas, feelings and their objects become dissociated. All that are left are mental objects as the objects of emotion, and ideas are no longer external. It becomes possible to consider whether the idea of God, for instance, refers to anything outside one's own mind. This results in the phenomenon of the conceit and other discordant metaphysical effects.

Eliot calls this the replacement of 'ontologism' by 'psychologism' or 'the whole pseudo-science of epistemology'.[11] This is the process described by Pope John Paul II as 'the decline of Thomistic' or Classical realism.[12]

The contemporary English theological school of Radical Orthodoxy describes it as the transition from ontology to epistemology: beginning soon after Aquinas, in the work of the Englishman Duns Scotus and culminating in Descartes.[13] Eliot shows how this process continues into the nineteenth and twentieth centuries in a comparison with the school of Baudelaire, in whose background a further deterioration had taken place in the mental landscape. In this school are included, along with Rimbaud, Eliot's poetic models, Jules Laforgue and Tristan Corbiere, and therefore Eliot himself. He felt this disintegration in himself, and saw it in his own work.[14]

Indeed it is possible that he never overcame it, despite his conversion to Anglo-Catholicism. He retained a divorce between his intellectual commitment to orthodoxy and his emotional commitment, as revealed in his poetry: what we might call a Protestant reserve. This progressive deterioration in the quality of metaphysical poetry between these three periods is also to be seen in different ways in non-metaphysical poetry. It is a consequence of the deterioration in the intellectual background, which he calls the 'disintegration of the intellect'. Integration had been achieved in the thirteenth century when religion, theology and mysticism; natural and moral philosophy; and personal feeling, as understood in the philosophy of love for instance, are in harmony and consistent with one another.[15]

In the thirteenth century, the theology and philosophy were those of Aquinas, the mysticism that of the Victorines, and the understanding of love was conveyed in the *Vita Nuova* of Dante, the love poetry of his friends, and in Chaucer's *Troilus and Criseyde*.[16] It derived from the Provençal, but it developed a great deal from there. In Italy it became orthodox and a part of medieval Christian rather than a pagan Latin Classical culture. Whereas the Provençal emphasized desire, which had to be adulterous, the Italian worshipped an ideal feminine beauty. The ideal was of contemplation and the superiority of their civil-ization was revealed in their poetic expression.[17] Decline was in part accidental, in part deliberate. But the consequence of the disintegration was the confusion of other activities such as science, politics or literary or artistic communication with belief.

When theology is no longer the central activity of a civilization these are no longer distinct and they become the objects of belief themselves: we see it in scientism, socialism or romanticism, for example. For Eliot, the poetic revolution had its intellectual origins in a certain type of Spanish Mysticism, which became the dominant mysticism of modern Catholicism, and its consequences for the poetry of Donne and his school. It was also associated with the development of the Protestant theology of Luther and Calvin, which emphasized the individual conscience, relationship with and feelings about God, rather than the grace that was sustained by the Church.

He identifies in the Jesuits' 'fine distinctions and discussions of conduct and casuisty' a new 'self-consciousness' not found in the Middle Ages.[18] He associates this with the 'Romanticism' of Ignatius, and of the Spanish Mystics, St Theresa, St John of the Cross, Luis of Granada and the Roman St Phillip Neri. He says they are as much 'psychologists as Descartes and Donne [and Luther] and as much romanticists as Rousseau'.[19] And he identifies the origins of this movement in the influence of 'Mohammedan' practices in Spain on St Ignatius, who was also 'a reader of romances'. It is thus 'non-Aristotelian' and 'outside of the Greco-Roman classical tradition'.[20] In the religious disorder of the sixteenth century he claimed they 'realised that an appeal to the sensibility is, for making converts, worth all your philosophy'.[21]

This 'Renaissance mysticism' is contrasted with the 'scholastic mysticism' of Richard and Hugh of St Victor 'which is taken up in the system of Aquinas'.[22] Their means and end are the same as that of Dante 'the divine contemplation, and the development and subsumption of emotion and feeling through intellect into the vision of God'.[23] The Spiritual

Exercises of Ignatius are by contrast 'a spiritual haschisch, a drugging of the emotions'.[24] He suggests that the origins of the theology of the sixteenth and seventeenth century are Augustinian not Thomist, though why this should be outside the Classical tradition is not clear.[25] The Victorines were also an Augustinian order, opposed in certain respects to Aquinas, as was Dante. He claimed an 'epistemological function for his poetry'[26] in opposition to Scholasticism which was opposed to the '*auctores* [classical authors], rhetoric, and poetry'.[27]

Nonetheless, the consequence for poetry was that, 'the sensuous interest of Donne in his own thoughts as objects' would lead him to the use of conceits.[28] In Donne one such idea is that 'strange... and possibly heretical idea' of the 'union, the fusion and identification of souls in sexual love' which is given 'sensible form', such as in *The Extasie*, *The Funerall* or *The Relique*.[29] This idea, of dubious orthodoxy, remains the central theme of the modern literature of love. In the first we see it clearly.

> When love, with one another so
>   Interinanimates two souls,
> That abler soul, which thence doth flow,
>   Defects of loneliness controls.

The possibility of the union of souls implies the separation of the soul and body, and thus the anxiety of the separation of the bodies.

> But O alas, so long, so far
>   Our bodies why do we forbear?
> They are ours, though they are not we, We are
>   The intelligences, they the sphere.

An anxiety expressed in such difficult images or conceits as this,

As 'twixt two equal Armies, Fate
  Suspends uncertain victory,
Our souls, (which to advance their state,
  Were gone out,) hung 'twixt her, and me.

And these, in which we see the whole modern Cartesian epistemological universe of sense-perception and scepticism, begin to unfold, ahead of time.

So must pure lovers souls descend
  T'affections, and to faculties,
Which sense may reach and apprehend,
  Else a great Prince in prison lies.
To our bodies turn we then, that so
  Weak men on love reveal'd may look;
Loves mysteries in souls doe grow,
  But yet the body is his book.
And if some lover, such as we,
  Have heard this dialogue of one,
Let him still mark us, he shall see
  Small change, when we are to bodies gone.

The thirteenth-century idea is of love as contemplation of the beauty of the other, and so as a partial revelation of absolute truth, beauty and goodness: 'contemplation of the beloved object' rather than 'the feelings and sensations of union'.[30] Eliot describes Dante's superior form of Metaphysical poetry as occurring in this form throughout the *Vita Nuova* and in another in the *Divine Comedy*. An example in the last canto of the *Paradiso* is the image of the shadow of the legendary first ship, the *Argo*, passing over the wondering Neptune. It is used to illustrate the wonder of the transitory moment that Dante gazes on the Eternal Light, the Beatific Vision of 'the Love that moves the sun and the other stars'.[31]

Nel suo profondo vidi che s'interna,
legato con amore in un volume,
ciò che per l'universo si squaderna:

sustanze e accidenti e lor costume
quasi conflati insieme, per tal modo
che ciò ch'i' dico è un semplice lume.

La forma universal di questo nodo
credo ch'i' vidi, perché più di largo,
dicendo questo, mi sento ch'i' godo.

Un punto solo m'è maggior letargo
che venticinque secoli a la 'mpresa
che fé Nettuno ammirar l'ombra d'Argo.

In its depth I saw that it contained, bound by love in one volume,
that which is scattered in leaves throughout the universe,

Substances and actions and their relations as if it were fused
together in such a way that what I tell of is a simple light.

I think I saw the universal form of this complex, because in
telling of it I feel my joy expand.

A single moment makes for me deeper oblivion than five and
twenty centuries upon the enterprise that made Neptune wonder
at the shadow of the Argo.[32]

In Dante the image is there to enhance our perception of
the feeling or idea, in Donne it becomes of interest in itself.[33]
Another example is from the second canto of the Paradiso,
where Dante evokes the experience of entering the first
heaven.

Parev' a me che nube ne coprisse
lucida, spessa, solida e pulita,
quasi adamante che lo sol ferisse.

Per entro sé l'etterna margarita
ne ricevette, com' acqua recepe
raggio di luce permanendo unita.

It seemed to me that a cloud enveloped us, shining, dense, firm
and polished, like a diamond struck by the sun.

Within itself the eternal pearl received us, as water doth receive
a ray of light, though still itself uncleft.[34]

It may not be simple but it is not meant to be of interest
in itself, rather it has 'a rational necessity'.[35] This is because
it is the incarnation of the philosophy, the theology and
the mysticism of the day, which is that of Scholasticism:
the incarnation in literature of these metaphysics. It is
metaphysical because it is explaining, or bringing into
the realm of the senses, something which is 'normally
apprehensible only by the intellect'. And it is done so in the
'clear, visual images' and ordinary language which were
taken up by the Modernists.[36] With Donne and his school
the clarity of Scholasticism is destroyed by the doctrinal
chaos of the Reformation. The nature of belief itself is
fundamentally altered by the process, that culminates in the
cogito, of making the objects of ideas psychological.

This 'toying' with ideas, images and feelings is
characteristic of the English Metaphysicals. Donne is more
inclined to toy with ideas such as that of the union of souls,
and Crashaw with feeling, especially religious feeling.[37]
Metaphysical poetry ends in English after the School of
Donne, as the sensibility is dissociated from the intellect.
Poetry becomes the expression of emotion divorced from
the intellect: philosophy is no longer accountable to the
emotions, and vice versa, hence the distortions of modern
literature and thought. This alteration in poetic image
shows the purest mode in which religion or metaphysical
belief is incarnated in literature, how the quality of that
literature is affected by the belief underlying the culture of
the time. It reveals the underlying 'metaphysical' status of
a culture. This status is revealed by the way in which ideas
are revealed in images, or as they deteriorate into conceits
and worse.

Meanwhile, Eliot reminds us that Dante is still the supreme guide to our inner, moral or spiritual, lives. The gradual ending of the medieval period would be defined by the waning of the influence of ecclesiastical Christianity, and its replacement by a multitude of other forms of belief. These included a privatized, personal version of Christianity, which was to lapse into an inevitable heterodoxy and latitudinarianism, and a number of other non-Christian substitutes. These are mostly versions of secular humanism that elevate particular aspects of human nature, such as individual faculties or principles of social organization such as reason or liberty, culminating in a privatized paganism. Dante and Chaucer are the supreme exemplars, in a continental and an insular form, of the situation prior to this decline. The English tradition was always more practical and the origins of later English popular anti-Catholicism, of 'No Popery', lay before the Reformation, in the anti-clericalism and English religious particularism of the Middle Ages.[38]

This derives from a distinctive English empiricism. It lacks the continental tradition of theological or devotional speculation and is rather a tradition of moderate, practical and even optimistic piety, which combines 'unimpeachable orthodoxy with individualism'.[39] The most authentic English witness to the truth of Christianity is that it *works*: that the teaching of Christ, his claim to be the Messiah and his moral teaching, is borne out in the lived experience of believers. It is this that justifies, or 'proves', the dogmas of the Incarnation, the Immaculate Conception and the Resurrection, for instance. They are essential to a belief whose moral truth is demonstrated by experience. Eliot believed that the psychological accuracy of the moral teachings of Christianity was the proof of its dogmas. As one of the fathers of the Second Vatican Council was to put it, 'no one has a doctrine so sublime and consonant with human nature as does the Church'.[40]

Chaucer's achievement was to encompass all of English

literature up to that point, and to assimilate it to ancient and contemporary continental tradition, especially French and Italian. Chaucer's particular literary achievement was to supersede the alliterative tradition and to integrate English into the mainstream of the new European literature. Chaucer like Dante was the author of the new vernacular literature itself.[41] He did so using the medieval techniques of rhetoric, of representing pre-existing material, as Dante did and Shakespeare too would do. Theirs was a culture where the classical was integrated with the Christian, a Holy Roman Empire whose temporal influence was to wane, but whose spiritual influence is, even now, undimmed. The literary significance of these writers is that they invented a literary vernacular tradition to rival the classical, and thus began the Classical tradition in vernacular literature. They created a vernacular that is neither autonomous nor insular, but adheres to shared European and classical standards, especially those transmitted through the Latin ecclesiastical tradition: indeed, until the interaction with Islamic civil-ization, this was the only means by which the classics were transmitted.

So this is where we begin and, although their achievement may have been matched in places, it has never been superseded. They wrote in the wake of the 'twelfth-century renaissance' and at the outset of the Renaissance proper, and while the latter phenomenon was to result in a fund-amental change of perspective whereby man rather than his maker became the measure of all things it was, as we have seen, also the 'outcome and flowerage' of the Middle Ages, and the 'crown of its achievement'.[42] Dante and Chaucer wrote at the outset of the modern world; which was also the end of the Roman; and as such they were on the cusp of the classical and the modern. This makes them the pivotal figures in the spiritual history of English and European Literature, the consummate, as well as the original, classical, Christian, European vernacular authors.

1. Curtius, Foreword to the English translation, *European Literature*, p. x.
2. Curtius, *European Literature*, p. 378.
3. Islamic knowledge of antiquity came from Byzantium and Alexandria.
4. Eliot, *Varieties of Metaphysical Poetry*, p. 222.
5. Derek Brewer, 'Medieval European Literature', p. 54.
6. Eliot, *Varieties of Metaphysical Poetry*, p. 176.
7. Humphrey Carpenter, *A Serious Character*, p. 258.
8. Eliot, *Varieties of Metaphysical Poetry*, p. 95.
9. Eliot, *Varieties of Metaphysical Poetry*, p. 54.
10. Eliot, *Varieties of Metaphysical Poetry,* p. 3.
11. Eliot, *Varieties of Metaphysical Poetry*, pp. 81–3.
12. John Paul II, *Memory and Identity,* p. 10.
13. See Milbank, Pickstock and Ward (eds), *Radical Orthodoxy*, pp. 5–6, 'the prising away of theology from ontology'; Pickstock, *After Writing*, p. 62, 'Descartes follows in the tradition of Duns Scotus'; and Philip Blond, 'Introduction', *Post-Secular Philosophy*, p. 6. The Pope is clearer, attributing the separation to Aquinas himself, see Joseph Ratzinger, *The Nature and Mission of Theology*, p. 16. Cowling's judgement on Milbank is that despite his socialism 'which stands out like a sanctified sore thumb ... [he]... does not capitulate to the post-Christian consensus' (*Religion and Public Doctrine*, vol. 3, p. 388).
14. See Chapter 7; Ackroyd, *T. S. Eliot*; and Joseph Bottum, 'What T. S. Eliot Almost Believed'.
15. Eliot, *Varieties of Metaphysical Poetry,* p. 78.
16. Eliot, *Varieties of Metaphysical Poetry,* p. 228 n., from *Times Literary Supplement* (19 August 1926).
17. Eliot, *Varieties of Metaphysical Poetry*, p. 94 n., 107–8 and 97.
18. Eliot, *Varieties of Metaphysical Poetry*, p. 80.
19. Eliot, *Varieties of Metaphysical Poetry*, p. 84. Neri founded the Oratorians which Newman and Manning joined in the nineteenth century when they converted. The Radical Orthodox account is that much of modern Roman Catholic theology and mysticism is a product of the separation of theology and philosophy after Aquinas as is Protestantism. For them as for Eliot the solution is to recover a situation when theology and philosophy are integrated: intellect and sensibility, mind and body. See Milbank, Theology and Social Theory.
20. Eliot, *Varieties of Metaphysical Poetry*, p. 75.
21. Eliot, *Varieties of Metaphysical Poetry*, pp. 162–3.
22. Eliot, *Varieties of Metaphysical Poetry,* p. 275.
23. Eliot, *Varieties of Metaphysical Poetry,* p. 103.
24. Eliot, *Varieties of Metaphysical Poetry*, p. 106.
25. Eliot, *Varieties of Metaphysical Poetry*, p. 276.
26. Curtius, *European Literature and the Latin Middle Ages*, p. 372.

27. Curtius, *European Literature and the Latin Middle Ages*, p. 224 and note 20: 'When Scholasticism speaks of beauty the word is used to indicate an attribute of God... Modern man immeasurably overvalues art because he has lost the sense of intelligible beauty that Neo-Platonism and the Middle Ages possessed.'

28. Eliot, *Varieties of Metaphysical Poetry*, p. 138: 'A conceit is the extreme limit of the simile and metaphor which is used for its own sake, and not to make clearer an idea or more definite an emotion.' Likewise, 'the conceited style is merely the development in poetry of an expository device known to preachers from the earliest times, the extended, detailed, interminable simile' (128–9).

29. Eliot, *Varieties of Metaphysical Poetry*, p. 111.

30. Eliot, V*arieties of Metaphysical Poetry*, p. 107.

31. Dante Alighieri, *Paradiso*, trans. Sinclair, p. 490.

32. Dante Alighieri, *Paradiso* XXXIII:85–96, trans. Sinclair, p. 483.

33. Eliot, *Varieties of Metaphysical Poetry*, p. 265.

34. Dante Alighieri, *Paradiso* II:31–6, cited at Eliot, *Varieties of Metaphysical Poetry*, pp. 120/265.

35. Eliot, *Varieties of Metaphysical Poetry*, p. 266.

36. Eliot, 'Dante', *Selected Prose*, p. 209.

37. Curtius, *European Literature*.

38. See Ackroyd, *Albion*, p. 127; and Norman, *Roman Catholicism*, pp. 4, 27, 119.

39. Ackroyd, *Albion*, p. 127.

40. Aidan Nichols, *Christendom Awake*, p. xii.

41. Ackroyd, *Albion*, pp. 154–5.

42. Eliot, V*arieties of Metaphysical Poetry*, pp. 162–3.

Chapter 4

The Puritan Cultural Revolution

The transition from 'ontologism' to 'psychologism' or epistemology, from Thomistic or Classical realism to Cartesianism, is incarnate in metaphysical poetry through the development of the rhetorical or conceited style. It is the transition from a culture of being to a culture of thought. Modern metaphysical poetry incarnates the *effect* of metaphysical ideas on the mind and emotions, rather than translating them into emotional terms in 'clear visual images'.[1] With the detachment of modern philosophical scepticism the sensibility becomes dissociated from those ideas. And so it is psychology, individual thought, imprecise feeling and belief rather than philosophical or theological ideas and the practice they embody that is incarnate in modern literature. Individual reason and experience become the ground of belief and practice as ecclesiastical Christianity is replaced by 'Paganism resurgent'.

In the previous chapter we saw how these metaphysical changes were incarnate in literature through the deterioration of metaphysical poetry and the 'disintegration of the intellect'. We also considered the greatest English medieval poet, perhaps the greatest of all English poets, Chaucer. The remainder of this book will show how the logical conclusion of the development of 'psychologism' or modern philosophy is the culture and the metaphysics of postmodernity: romantic, relativist, solipsistic, nihilist and existentialist. In the next chapter we shall see how the metaphysical changes between the medieval and modern world were incarnate in the development of prosody: the development of a more and more complex syllabic metre from the accentual, alongside the deterioration of the intellectual and emotional content. The introduction of continental and classical forms transformed the alliterative prosody native to the Germanic origins of the English language, without perpetuating the Latin Classical tradition from which these forms derived.

But first we consider the most powerful literary incarnation of the metaphysical revolution, as Dante and Chaucer were the most powerful incarnation of the situation before it: Shakespeare. The deterioration that Eliot saw in metaphysical poetry, as a consequence of the 'disintegration of the intellect', was extended to all literary forms, through the 'dissociation of the sensibility' after Shakespeare and Donne.[2] As philosophy was dissociated from theology and the entire view of every aspect of life that it implies, so the understanding of private emotion and behaviour was divorced from thought. The cultural history of the Reformation is that of the incarnation of a metaphysical transformation in literary form, in the literature of the Renaissance. But it is also incarnate in musical and visual form, through the development of polyphony from plainsong, the emergence of modern art from the destruction of the idols and the 'Stripping of the Altars'.[3]

The Puritan Cultural Revolution was the consummation of a political coup. Through it the religion and culture of the English people was transformed, by an elite acting in its own self-interest. The nursery rhyme 'Little Jack Horner' is exemplary. It is supposed to refer to the material gains of a certain class at the seizure of lands at the dissolution which inclined many of them later to the Parliamentary and Whig causes. 'Jack' or rather Thomas Horner supposedly helped himself to one of twelve deeds he was supposed to deliver to Henry VIII, hidden in a pie. The plum was Mells Manor in Somerset.[4] The Puritan Cultural Revolution was the political and cultural incarnation of a religious doctrine developed for sectional rather than universal interests. Sir Francis Bacon shows how far this religious commitment became a scientific, philosophical, political and economic commitment, which is alive and well.[5]

It began with the exploitation of Lutheran and Erastian ideas, building on Wycliffian biblicism and the background of medieval Gallicianism or particularism, all of which derived from a native English empiricism, pragmatism and exceptionalism. These were used by Henry VIII and Thomas Cramner for political purposes: the 'one definite thing that can be said about the Reformation in England is that it was an act of State'. This opened the way for the ensuing theological and then ideological 'complexity and lack of clarity'.[6] The Puritan Cultural Revolution ended with the influence of neo-Platonist Renaissance Roman Catholic thinkers, which became the theology of the confessional state of 1688 to 1829. The Cambridge Platonists held that true authority in religion resided in the individual conscience, and the religion which might guide it. Revelation was thus subsumed into natural religion or paganism.[7]

The Church of England thus became a 'broad church' through the Arminian rejection of Calvinism: which 'preserved the intense moral seriousness of Puritanism, but dropped its characteristic theological justification of that seriousness in the doctrines of grace and predestination'.[8] The result was the moral self-righteousness of modern political dogma and a personal credulity or secular superstition. The replacement of theology by 'rational' philosophy was the means by which neo-paganism crept back in. The Protestant confessional state, the Whig aristocracy that lasted from 1688 until 1829, was the political incarnation of this sceptical moralizing latitudinarianism. It was the entrenchment of a lapsed version of the Commonwealth that was to become the secular confessional state. The latter was the result of the democratic reforms demanded by religious pluralism: dissent against the eighteenth century confessional state.[9]

So, the intervening period, the story of the rise and fall of the Puritans, or Calvinism, was critical. It was the defining event of the Reformation in England and in the emergence of 'Anglo-Saxon' modernity. It secured the demise of the Latin Classical tradition in England and the marginalization of Catholic or universal Christianity in national life. It is no accident that its origins were in Switzerland, with its Celtic or 'barbarian' heritage, as were those of Lutheranism in Eastern Germany. Despite the liberal Catholic outward appearance, clothing or dress of the Church of England, Calvinism is central to its doctrinal orthodoxy, as contained within the Thirty-nine Articles. They are patristic regarding the the Trinity, Christology and original sin; Lutheran regarding the Gospel and justification; and Calvinist regarding the sacraments.[10] Central too is the Calvinist Evangelical party whose place within the Church remains essential.[11]

Calvinism transformed the idea of a Chosen People into one in which the elect was only a part of the Chosen nation, or, in its dealings with the wider world, only a part of humanity.[12] Those whose election was predestined was revealed by outward signs such as moral rectitude, material success and conspicuous works of charity. It was the climax of reformed Christianity, after which there was decay. It lapsed into latitudinarianism, the religion of the individual conscience, when it was found to be impossible. But its moral force remains with us in the remnants of the morality of decency and respectability in English and other modern, capitalist societies. In its moral authoritarianism and capitalist materialism it becomes rational liberalism or secular humanism: the religion of the individual conscience. The content of its belief, its view of the individual relationship with God, is that it is private.[13] Its content can become almost anything, within the bounds of social, which means secular liberal, acceptability.

As soon as material success became the emblem of election we are into the modern secular materialist world. It was the triumph of the secular or earthly city; and its chief success was the foundation of the first secular state, or states: France and the United States. There the sacred and the state are fused just as they were in the pagan world and the constant talk is of the consecration of the secular. The emergence of the secular or deist version in the eighteenth century lies behind the secular political constitutions and secular political religions of France (which skipped Protestantism and went straight from Catholicism to Infidelity) and the United States, and the many other modern political states, assumptions and creeds that they have influenced. And they are as much political religions as those of Russia or Germany were in the twentieth century, and they are as far from orthodox ecclesiastical Christianity, and as destructive of it, as medieval heresy.[14]

England had been central to the establishment and the continuation of the Latin Classical tradition. But now the anti-Latin party had taken over, while Celtic Ireland preserved its Catholicism.[15] The emergence of England as a nation-state was already almost a thousand years past, but now it was transformed into a spiritual and cultural island. It became isolated from Europe and it proceeded to spread this new culture around the world, in competition with Iberian Catholic Imperialism. Similar changes were to take place in the other countries of the Latin world, in France and Spain and Italy, but in England the coup predated them by centuries.[16] The English and Dutch took a reformed idea of themselves as a Chosen People sent from God to bring the benefits of civilization around the world. Protestantism became associated with the idea of material success and democracy, and Catholicism with monarchy and backwardness.

The metaphysical transformation that T. S. Eliot and John Paul II describe from an Anglo- and a Roman Catholic perspective is approached from another by Ted Hughes. As an anthropologist as well as a poet and writer he was interested in myth and magic as well as religion and poetry: albeit from the perspective of secular academic anthropology. The former are concerned with the epistemological problem of modernity, which arises in characteristic form from the *cogito*: that the starting point of thought and therefore belief is the self, and the revolutionary consequences this has for religion and culture. While lacking the ecumenical sensitivities or the philosophical and theological background of the others, Hughes is more specific in the role that he ascribes to Puritanism, as the herald and avant-garde of the age of scepticism and reason. Eliot may also, as we shall see, have had personal reasons to avoid it.[17]

What Hughes describes is the moment of birth of the modern world from the Catholicism or paganism of the Middle Ages and before. He describes it as a severance from something that is essential to a wholeness or 'complete being', in which intellect and sensibility and soul are integrated. He sees this severance as something achieved by Puritanism, or started by it and completed by the secular rationalism that followed. The soul became understood, if at all, in materialist terms as the ego of psychology, or the subject of philosophy: materialist superstitions replacing spiritual beliefs. This story is the underlying plot of the English Reformation and of Shakespeare's plays and so the underlying story of subsequent English literature. The English Reformation was a religious rejection of a wholeness or completeness of being, and of culture, of art and literature.

This is visible in the relegation of religion to books and prayers, the destruction of icons and statues, and liturgy, the end of pilgrimages and holy days: of an incarnate faith, rather than one of the mind.[18] Hughes sees the problem as that of excessive rationality and divorce from the instinctive, physical, emotional and sacred aspects of our humanity: 'complete being'. This wholeness or 'Goddess' was destroyed by Puritanism and the spirit of rationalism and individualism that worked through it. He also sees it in prosody, with Wyatt as the turning point at which the orthodox (accentual-syllabic) took over from the unorthodox metre (alliterative or accentual). In unorthodoxy is 'an insistent, peculiar subjective factor – an instinctive attempt to include the experience that orthodoxy excludes, a spontaneous attempt to find direct expression for balanced wholeness of being'.

The new 'Classical' syllabic prosody was associated with the defence of the new Puritan or rationalist orthodoxy (which may also infect modern Catholicism).[19] It is a spiritual and metaphysical transformation incarnate in literary form. But where did this new spirit come from, that resulted in the emergence of modernity, from the Renaissance, the Reformation and the Enlightenment? It was always there but it was liberated by the material changes made possible by the scientific and technological development that began in the early Renaissance. The encounter with Islam had a number of stimulating effects. In Spain, the work of the twelfth-century Moor Averroes, '*the* commentator' on Aristotle, reintroduced him into the European tradition, which allowed Aquinas and Scholasticism to develop.[20] Also, the Islamic Empire centred on Baghdad had a more advanced scientific culture at the time.

It had preserved some ancient learning that had been lost in the West, and introduced the decimal system and 'Arabic' numerals from India, which encouraged the development of modern science. We have already seen the effect of Islamic models on Spanish Mysticism and another development was the establishment of the universities in the twelfth century on Islamic models. V. S. Naipaul in his visits to Islamic universities in Iran describes the peculiar experience of seeing scholars wearing the same gowns he had first encountered at Oxford.[21] All these developments lead ultimately to challenges to the historic power and authority of Rome and its successor the Church. They encouraged the growth of the independent power and authority of reason, the individual and the nation, alongside gradual economic growth.

In other words, they strengthened and emboldened the centrifugal forces. Traditional Christianity was replaced with new forms of Christianity, which were less offensive to this new spirit, and later on new sub-cults and religions of the individual, of reason, and of the nation. The consequence of this was to liberate the innate human tendency to exalt the self and thus to denigrate the idea of dependence on a creator God, or an institution designed to propagate that idea. The development of science and technology had a number of moral, psychological and spiritual consequences, which constituted the 'disintegration of the intellect'. Printing was the final weapon that this process required, and the crisis began in England.

Hughes applies the anthropological framework of Shamanism to Western Literature and culture. For Hughes great writers, including Shakespeare and Eliot and others such as Yeats and Isaac Bashevis Singer may be seen as great literary shamen. He tells us that when a culture or people is threatened with destruction a great shaman tends to appear. Thus Isaac Bashevis Singer was the shaman of 'East European Hasidic Jewry', while Eliot was the shaman of the 'spiritual tradition of the West' threatened with destruction by the 'scientific materialism of the American economic miracle'.[22] Yeats was a 'Gnostic or unorthodox' version of this, while Shakespeare incarnated the conflict between Puritanism 'together with its accompanying materialist and democratising outlook and rational philosophy...' and the Goddess religion of medieval Catholicism: he was the shaman of both.[23] And Milton, Blake and Wordsworth would be later versions of this same 'new spirit' or 'revolutionary sensibility' which 'locates the new order not on a spiritual plane but on earth, in social forms'.[24]

Shakespeare incarnated both the persecuting Puritan, who destroys himself in the process, and the suffering of the Goddess.[25] This was the 'civil war' which took place in every soul in Shakespeare's lifetime and became a real civil war soon after.[26] It is the fundamental plot or 'ground plan' of his plays, the 'tragic equation'. This plot always contains 'two myths – of the Great Goddess and of the Goddess-destroying god', the '"madness" of the Puritan fear of sexuality'.[27] It becomes 'an equation where the first half, by its own inherent dynamics, produces the second half...

always producing the same tragic explosion'.[28] And the same Goddess, 'female sexuality as a symbol of the Mother of Creation – in a Christianized form opened to Dante the ultimate vision of his *Paradiso*'.[29] In ancient Greece too the Goddess had been destroyed by 'a pragmatic, sceptical, moralizing, desacralizing spirit': that of Socrates.[30]

Hughes thus extends his account of prosody, associating classical or continental syllabic metre with Puritanism, and the severance Puritanism represented from the wholeness which is to be found in native speech and rhythms, and associated with Catholicism or paganism. He concurs with Eliot in that way that it describes the literature that emerges from the Civil War as lacking something that was there before. Hughes's analysis is influenced by feminism and other secular ideologies that are the consequence of the deterioration that he describes, not least the secular discipline of anthropology.[31] He also echoes the mythic psychology of Jung as well as other hermetic or 'New Age' accounts.[32]

But the rationalism that is associated with Puritanism and the rejection of ecclesiastical Christianity or ancient pagan religion does not destroy the human need for belief, the religious sense. What it does is to translate it into political or other modern 'world-immanent' causes such as socialism, or liberalism, or humanitarianism; or alternatively into superstitions, such as spiritualism, and other new age, hermetic or esoteric phenomena, such as Kabbala or horoscopes. And Hughes's account of the 'Goddess' is echoed by Curtius: for him too she is 'one of the last religious experiences of the late-pagan world',[33] who has always been associated with literature (rather than philosophy or theology) but was submerged throughout much of the Latin Middle Ages. And she re-emerged in the Renaissance with the occult neo-platonism of Pico della Mirandola whom Hughes describes as inspiring Shakespeare.[34] This was also behind the development of the broad church Whiggery of the eighteenth century. The Cambridge Platonists were an

Anglican version of the same thing. Both tried to synthesize 'Christianity and Greek intellectual mysticism, with a dose of the Jewish mysticism of the Kabbala thrown in for good measure'.[35]

One work revealed this hidden stream during the Christian era: the *De universitate mundi*, 'On The Universe', divided into the *Megacosmus* and the *Microcosmus*, of Bernard Silvestris of Tours. Curtius describes it as 'a link in the "golden chain" which connects late Paganism with the Renaissance of the twelfth century'. It results in the Grail and courtly romances in which 'Ancient vegetation cults' merged with 'the symbolism of the Eucharist and survived esoterically into the Middle Ages'.[36] It is the theme that underlies that history and the history of modern literature: the opposition between the values of the Church and those of classical literature. The supreme achievements of Western culture are those in which that opposition is transcended: in which the achievements of Greece, Rome and Israel are consummated.

This is the creative symbiosis that Curtius describes as leading from antiquity through the Latin Middle Ages, and into the vernacular literatures of modern Europe. The Enlightenment, which was the consequence of Puritanism and Latitudinarianism, was the means by which Paganism was revived. But the consequence of this was not a classical literature, for this was not based on a revival of the pagan religions of Greece and Rome, but Romanticism, and before it Neo-classicism. Rationalism bred irrationalism. While the Enlightenment dreamt that reason would rid the world of superstition and priests, in fact it encouraged them, through the new priesthood of writers, the proclaimers of liberty and other earthly doctrines, and the gurus of the 'new (post-Christian) age'.

The Enlightenment, which was supposed to be a response to the intellectual darkness of revealed religion, liberated modern Europe from the Latin Classical tradition, as the Reformation did for ecclesiastical Christianity. This is the process we shall see in the development of literary movements, which are both artistic movements and incarnations of post-ecclesiastical Christian doctrines. The Enlightenment, which was supposed to be a liberation from the intellectual darkness of revealed religion, became a re-enslavement to Paganism. First, of the political 'heaven-on-earth' variety, such as led to the French and American Revolutions, Nazism and Communism, and second of the superstitious, supernatural, or individualistic variety, that were the consequence of these creeds. When people were freed to believe anything they wanted, they would do just that. Reason became the vehicle by which the intellectual darkness of a new paganism was loosed on the modern world, whether it took a collectivist or individualist form. Its literary incarnation was first Neoclassical then Romantic, Modernist then Postmodernist.

---

1. Eliot, *Varieties of Metaphysical Poetry*, p. 202. Eliot described this as the 'objective correlative' of the emotion: 'in the best of the metaphysical poetry there is exactness; the object of feeling is always definite'.
2. Eliot, *Selected Prose*, pp. 64–6. He was later to retract this specific attribution of responsibility to Milton and Dryden ('Milton II' [1947], Selected Prose, pp. 265–74), cited Eliot, 'Introduction', *Varieties of Metaphysical Poetry*, p. 29. Dissociation implies the impossibility of metaphysical poetry.
3. The story of the emergence of polyphony is told in the opera *Palestrina*, by Hans Pfitzner; the story of the development of British art out of the destruction of the idols by Andrew Graham-Dixon in *History of British Art*, and the ecclesiastical history by Eamon Duffy, in *Stripping of the Altars*.
4. Although this account is disputed by the family.
5. See Kenneth Hopper and William Hopper, *The Puritan Gift*.
6. Sir Maurice Powicke, *The Reformation in England*, p. 1, cited Aidan Nichols, *Panther and the Hind*, p. 21. It is thus 'the most complex and heterogeneous – if also, arguably, the least religiously warranted – of the ecclesiastical revolutions of the sixteenth century... the variableness of Anglican theology... derives from that complexity – and lack of clarity' (Nichols, *Panther and the Hind*, 1–2).
7. Nichols, *Panther and the Hind*, p. 86; also see Pico della Mirandola below.
8. Nichols, Panther and the Hind, pp. 83–4.

9. Norman, *Anglican Difficulties*, p. 74.

10. Nichols, *Panther and the Hind*, p. 33.

11. Nichols, *Panther and the Hind*, p. 103.

12. Nichols, *Panther and the Hind*, pp. 31–2.

13. Norman, *Anglican Difficulties*, p. 86. 'Making up the content of religion for oneself, after all, is what the Anglican churches have been doing for centuries' (148).

14. For American religion as more Gnostic than orthodox ecclesiastical Christian, see Harold Bloom, *American Religion*: 'We think we are Christian but we are not' he writes 'even our secularists indeed even our professed atheists, are more Gnostic than humanist in their ultimate propositions' (p. 22). This view is derived from that of Emerson and William James. Leo XIII's encyclical of 1899, *Testem Benevolentiae Nostrae*, warns of the dangers of 'those... views called by some "Americanism"'. It also implied criticism of France. For the French Revolution and other political religions, see Michael Burleigh, *Earthly Powers*.

15. Thus becoming like the picture to England's Dorian Gray

16. See Burleigh, *Earthly Powers*; and Edward Norman, T*he Roman Catholic Church*.

17. See Chapter 6, for his own Puritan background and the fact that orthodox Anglo-Catholicism was thriving then as it has been destroyed now.

18. See Duffy, *Stripping of the Altars*; Graham-Dixon, *History of British Art*; Hughes, *Winter Pollen*, p. 375.

19. Hughes, *Winter Pollen*, p. 374; see also Chapter 4 (Hughes, *Winter Pollen*, pp. 320–75). The oddity of this scheme, which may make sense in an English or Anglo-Saxon context, is that orthodoxy is the Protestant or modern orthodoxy, which is in fact the denial of Christian orthodoxy, while Catholicism is identified with paganism: the Goddess and balanced wholeness. But it accords with Pugin who identified the Gothic, or non-Classical, with 'Christian Architecture' and saw the neo-Classical or neo-Pagan as a travesty of it, incarnating the new rationalist, pagan spirit.

20. Roger Scruton, *A Short History of Modern Philosophy*.

21. Naipaul, *Beyond Belief*, p. 217.

22. Hughes, *Shakespeare and the Goddess of Complete Being*, p. 89.

23. Hughes, *Winter Pollen*, p. 110.

24. Hughes, *Shakespeare and the Goddess of Complete Being*, p. 90.

25. Hughes, *Shakespeare and the Goddess of Complete Being*, pp. 91–2.

26. Hughes, *Winter Pollen*, pp. 108–10.

27. Hughes, *Shakespeare and the Goddess of Complete Being*, p. 2.

28. Hughes, *Shakespeare and the Goddess of Complete Being*, pp. 1–15

29. Hughes, *Shakespeare and the Goddess of Complete Being*, p. 4.

30. Hughes, *Shakespeare and the Goddess of Complete Being*, p. 85; and

Hughes, *Winter Pollen*, p. 212.

31. This is a theme taken up by modern feminists in challenging the authority of the Magisterium. It also forms part of the background to the ordination of women in the Church of England. See William Oddie, *The Roman Option*, pp. 122–4, for the relationship between feminism, the neo-pagan 'goddess movement' and women priests.

32. As does Curtius's method of seeking continual recurrences of aspects of antique rhetoric and indeed Christopher Booker's method in his *The Seven Basic Plots*.

33. Curtius, *European Literature and the Latin Middle Ages*, p. 106.

34. Hughes, S*hakespeare and the Goddess of Complete Being*, p. 20.

35. Nichols, *Panther and the Hind*, pp. 86–7.

36. Curtius, *European Literature and the Latin Middle Ages*, pp. 111–12.

Chapter 5

Neoclassicism

Do you think he is so unskilful in his craft, as to ask you openly and plainly to join him in his warfare against the Truth? No; he offers you baits to tempt you. He promises you civil liberty; he promises you equality; he promises you trade and wealth; he promises you a remission of taxes; he promises you reform. This is the way in which he conceals from you the kind of work to which he is putting you; he tempts you to rail against your rulers and superiors; he does so himself, and induces you to imitate him; or he promises you illumination,—he offers you knowledge, science, philosophy, enlargement of mind. He scoffs at times gone by; he scoffs at every institution which reveres them. He prompts you what to say, and then listens to you, and praises you, and encourages you. He bids you mount aloft. He shows you how to become as gods. Then he laughs and jokes with you, and gets intimate with you; he takes your hand, and gets his fingers between yours, and grasps them, and then you are his.

(John Henry Newman, Tracts for the Times, Tract 83 [1838])

We have seen how the metaphysical, theological, or ideological transformation, the replacement of a culture of being by a culture of thought that occurred during the Reformation was incarnate in the literature of the Renaissance. God was replaced as the starting point of all things, the basic assumption, by man, by the individual; first in theology, then in philosophy and then in politics and culture. The result was the attempt to deny revelation and the supernatural through reason. Christianity was replaced by rationalism and paganism was let in through the back door. Pagan and Jewish literature had been incorporated into and transmitted through the Latin Classical tradition, but the new paganism was no longer Classical. Literature went from being the incarnation of Christian metaphysics to being the incarnation of spiritual individualism, heterodoxy and heresy. Metaphysical poetry was eclipsed by Neoclassicism and the Romantic Hellenism which went on to replace it. This was for Eliot the 'dissociation of the sensibility' from the intellect, of poetry from thought, part of a wider 'disintegration of the intellect', and for Hughes the 'final loss of the creative soul'. The theological term for the inspiration for the cult of the individual that this became, according to Newman, is Satan.

In this chapter we see how this was incarnate in poetic form, from Chaucer and the sub-Chaucerians, the Elizabethans and Stuarts, to the Augustans, 'pre-romantics' and Romantics proper.[1] The late medieval influence of contemporary foreign vernaculars, on Chaucer and his followers became the direct modern influence of the classics: through translation, imitation and original composition. This was a dissociation from the natural music of the language. We also see the emergence of a 'more mature prose'[2] out of the poetic foundations of English and European literature, in which perhaps its greatest achievements had been. So the development of prose, both fiction and non-fiction, is related to this metaphysical development. A vigorous vernacular prose literature emerges at the same time as literacy becomes more widespread, in part as a consequence of printing. First hand-printing and then machine-printing were associated with the Reformation and the mass education and literacy of the Industrial Revolution.

It is associated therefore with the rise of democratic and non-ecclesiastical values. Prose, first non-fiction and then fiction, begins to emerge as a rival to poetry as a literary form in English. Although Latin was preferred for learning, there had been specific forms of vernacular prose literature in the Middle Ages. This started with Alfred, and included sermons, saints' lives, histories and translations, while devotional books and tracts continued to be important through the Reformation. After the Norman Conquest, it was not until the eighteenth century that prose vernacular literature began to rival poetry as a vehicle of literature: the same time that the Latin Classical tradition lost its authority to the idea of individual creativity.

So, the initial reaction to the 'disintegration' or desacralization was the attempt to reverse it: to recreate, revive or reconstruct the Latin Classical tradition by recreating it in English. However, this attempt occurred at the same time as the Enlightenment began: one might even say that it was an Enlightenment project. This attempt was accompanied and undermined therefore by a continued development away from medieval metaphysics, incarnate in the subsequent emergence of 'Romantic Hellenism' out of this late Renaissance Latinity.[3] These were thus the first in a number of movements, periods, reactions and counter-reactions, from Neoclassicism and Romanticism to Modernism and Postmodernism, which have characterized the period since the break up of the Latin Classical tradition and ecclesiastical Christianity. They represent spiritual as much as literary or artistic characteristics.

As Eliot put it in his first poetic manifesto, *Reflections on Vers Libre* in 1917, 'In modern society such revolutions are almost inevitable... tradition is ever lapsing into superstition, and the violent stimulus of novelty is required.'[4] Later, he would add '[w]hat is objectionable... is not novelty or originality in themselves, but their glorification for their own sake';[5] that we are no longer 'born and brought up in the environment of a living and central tradition';[6] or rather that the 'central and living tradition' is no longer that of ecclesiastical Christianity and the Latin Classical tradition. Instead it is that of liberal individualism, of secular humanism, which has become a religion in itself, and is defined by the denial or the subjectivity, the relativity, of tradition. The existence of a tradition, an external cultural or spiritual authority to which the individual would submit, would be at odds with the spirit and practice of this belief. It is a cycle therefore from which we have never escaped and so defines the modern period. Each movement represents a tendency in literature and thought, which becomes exaggerated and distorted, in the absence of the balance provided by a coherent and stable spiritual and thus cultural context.

The influence of the Latin Classical tradition has been denied by the emphasis on individual creativity, by Romanticism, and that is the reason for the demise of literature. We are ready then for a re-engagement, a revival of the influence of that tradition, which has declined with the decline of ecclesiastical Christianity, in England in particular, but in the Western world in general. This is therefore a revival of the sense of tradition in general as well as of a particular tradition, as opposed to the cult of the individual. This is the distinguishing feature of the religion of art that is the particular incarnation of the secular humanism or paganism that is associated with romanticism. It is the consequence of the rationalist rejection of revelation, which we examine in the next chapter. But for now we see the emergence of the process where the individual creative writer or artist has had to establish their identity and position in a self-conscious way, to establish the spiritual and cultural tradition within which they operate.

From Dryden to Johnson we see the beginnings of this process, and we also see recent attempts to do so, by Ted Hughes and T. S. Eliot. This self-creation and need to establish a tradition within which the writer is working is characteristic of the modern situation, where there is no 'central and living tradition'. The relationship between memory and creation is fundamental, between knowledge of the tradition and its reinvention: acts of creative remembering. This is at the heart of Curtius's argument about the way in which classical literature was transmitted through the Church into modern literature, and the way in which modern writers should understand their inheritance and themselves. 'The literary tradition is the means by which the European mind preserves its identity through the millenniums... [yet] Much must be forgotten if the essential is to be preserved.'[7] It was only at the very end of the ancient world, in obscurity, that the concept of the 'creative imagination' had appeared, in Longinus and Macrobius, where it derived from the influence of the idea of the 'legislator of the Jews' and the cult of Virgil.[8]

It would take another fifteen centuries for this 'theological metaphor' of the 'creative mind' to re-emerge.[9] Curtius describes the emergence of modern lyric poetry out of the ancient forms, through the setting of words to music in the eighth-century Church. In addition to the two poetic systems that Hughes describes as orthodox and unorthodox, classical prose was regulated by rhythm. But in the liturgy a form developed in which a text was set to music with as many syllables as the respective section of the melody had notes: 'this text had no connection with either metrical or rhythmical verse, but was pure prose, and in France it was, and still is, so called'.[10] Thereby poets and writers of prose were freed from the small number of traditional forms. In addition to the emergence of the rhythmic aspect of the vernacular lyric, at the same time 'Rhyme – as foreign to the Romans as to the Germanic peoples' was introduced.

Thus the modern vernacular lyric is composed of different elements from the classical forms, and the direct influence of the classical forms after the Reformation was of a different order of influence from that of the sister vernaculars before it. The Latin Classical tradition was one of the perpetuation of tradition by its recreation but the Restoration saw the introduction of a new type of Classicism from France. Whereas Chaucer had introduced forms from within a common culture, and was creating an English literature out of both languages and traditions, there was now a direct import of Classical forms into English, which conflicted with the natural music of the language. Coleridge, in his *Biographia Literaria* describes the school of Pope as 'that school of French poetry, condensed and invigorated by English understanding'. It was a further divorce from the prosody natural to the

English language from that unity achieved by Chaucer and Shakespeare, and the new prose style was artificial too.[11]

Hughes describes the Restoration as the moment at which the court imposed French tastes on a nation whose radical Englishness it had good reason to fear. The prose of the Elizabethans and Carolines was replaced by that of Addison and the new artificial speech code was that which was subsequently transported around the world as the Queen's English. In prosody Ted Hughes likens the relationship to a 'cartoonish' marriage where 'the old or unorthodox tradition is the bride and the new, metrically strict orthodox tradition is the groom'. The honeymoon is with Chaucer, then the story moves on to Wyatt ('difficulties, the first spats') and Surrey ('his sudden severity'), Marlowe and Shakespeare ('she erupts', 'he fights to subdue her'), Milton ('they live in the same house but separated', this is the moment of the dissociation), Restoration ('she fell into the gutter'), French Revolution ('she fell into the arms of Blake, Wordsworth and Coleridge'), Tennyson ('became the official mourner, over his nightly port') and Hopkins ('followed her... through Wales and into Ireland').[12]

Thomas Wyatt was on the cusp of the syllabic and accentual tradition: the conflict between orthodox and unorthodox metre had been at its most intense in the conflict between his work and that of his editors. The transition in his verse from unorthodox or accentual to orthodox, or syllabic (as embodied in Spenser) is seen in the efforts of editors, like Tottel, to constrain or liberate his counterpointed music.[13] The suppression of the unorthodox form occurred at the same time as the Puritan Cultural Revolution, and its establishment of the new religious orthodoxy. The former is the tradition that Hughes and others set about recovering: by rediscovering the natural music of the language, unfettered by the demands of conventional prosody, liberated by the experiments of Coleridge and Hopkins, and, in another mode, by Pound and Eliot.[14] It has its counterpart in the attempt to liberate the Latin Classical tradition from the Protestant and Puritan culture which succeeded and suppressed it. This had undermined the creative fusion of the traditions of Israel, Greece and Rome, that was the central creative force in European culture. This dissociation from the native music of the language was begun before the Civil War, and was completed afterwards. It was thus the formal or prosodic counterpart of the dissociation of the sensibility from the intellect. Hughes addresses the problem of identifying the nature of the spiritual meaning of the various verse forms, of their traditions and exemplars, the metaphysic that they incarnated. The new syllabic orthodoxy was the means by which the new religion undermined the creative fusion of the pagan and Catholic that was the Latin Classical tradition, and had been the native music of the language and the people until the Civil War. Neoclassicism was the consummation of the introduction of syllabic regularity, through imitation of classical rather than continental metre, which had been begun with Chaucer and was reinvigorated by Wyatt. It was syllabic, but it was not yet marked by the formalism which Eliot found in the nineteenth century, in Swinburne, for example.

> The English ear is (or was) more sensitive to the music of verse and less dependent upon the recurrence of identical sounds in [iambic pentameter] than in any other... it is possible that excessive devotion to rhyme has thickened the modern ear... [15]

Neoclassicism was the introduction, imitation and translation not only of themes but also of values: the classical values of decorum, restraint and respect for the Latin Classical tradition. But it mistook the surface of that tradition for its essence: a creative literature contained within the metaphysical boundaries set by ecclesiastical Christianity. Thus while Eliot had followed Johnson's definition of the English Metaphysical poets, he disagreed with some of Johnson's judgements, and he also disagreed with him about

vernacular in opposition to Latin Classical literature.[25] Indeed the whole subject of English Literature as an academic discipline assumes this Romantic framework of a self-sufficient vernacular. The irony was that the living embodiment of antiquity, Greek as much as Roman, was the Roman Catholic Church and the Latin Classical tradition in literature.[26]

The escape from the latter, into a Hellenistic one, and beyond, was a deliberate avoidance of the medieval ecclesiastical tradition, with all its metaphysical implications. It was the direct appreciation of another which had been in part mediated through Rome and the Latin Classical tradition, but also through Islamic Spain. The Romantic reaction to Neoclassicism thus reflected a reaction, reflected too in the evangelical and charismatic movement, to Enlightenment reason, which was identified with the formality of Augustan poetry. The Neoclassical movement was committed to something metaphysical which was in conflict with the Enlightenment. Each was equally a part of and a reaction to it, and a step away from medieval 'integration'.

Romanticism attempted to find in a poetry that related to the language and concerns of the 'people' a response to so-called Classicist artifice. This was seen as a divorce from the language of common speech, and so they were seen to align themselves with the popular and radical movements of the day. Their emphasis was on the vernacular. However, the Neoclassicist movement, as we have seen, was itself in opposition to the *ancien regime*, the Whig aristocracy which dominated the confessional state from 1688 to 1832, and the Protestant rationalizing spirit they embodied. They were trying to preserve something which had almost been lost, whereas the Whigs were embracing the new, and finally 'in the 1790s the Jacobin agenda obscured the Jacobite one'.[27]

Poetry thus represented a dual opposition, from left and from right, antagonistic to Enlightenment or eighteenth-century rationalism. They were opposed in their view of a solution as coming from the past or a revolutionary future: the alternatives were feeling or classical order. Both were the consequence of the dissociation of sensibility from the intellect. One form was rational, the other emotional. Neoclassicism was concurrent with the Enlightenment, and Romanticism a development out of it. Augustan poetry began rational and classical and ended emotional: it began Neoclassical and ended Romantic. It was a mixture of the rejection and the embrace of reason: each, in its own way, a departure from the Latin Classical tradition, and ecclesiastical Christianity: one regretting and one rejoicing in that change.

----

1. Curtius, *European Literature and the Latin Middle Ages*, p. 270.

2. Eliot, *The Function of Criticism'*, Selected Prose,p. 72

3. Cf. Stern, *The Rise of Romantic Hellenism in English Literature 1732–1786*, cited by Clark, *Samuel Johnson*, p. 251.

4. Eliot, 'Reflections on Vers Libre', *New Statesman* (3 March 1917), repr. Eliot, *Selected Prose*, p. 32.

5. T. S. Eliot, *After Strange Gods*, p. 23.

6. Eliot, *After Strange Gods*, quoted in Cowling, *Religion and Public Doctrine*, vol. 1, p. 111.

7. Curtius, *European Literature and the Latin Middle Ages*, pp. 395–6. Note the influence of Goethe, Kant and post-Kantian German philosophy on Wordsworth and the neo-pagan idea that emerged of the poet's creativity as the 'same force which operates in external nature' (397).

8. Curtius, *European Literature and the Latin Middle Ages*, pp. 146 and 400.

9. With it comes the danger of an excess of forgetfulness and a sanctification of the individual creative faculty or personality. This is what drove Curtius to write his book, in Nazi Germany: sharing with John Paul II and Benedict XVI direct experience of the radical materialism of Nazism or Communism.

10. Karl Streker, cited by Curtius, *European Literature and the Latin Middle Ages*, pp. 150–1.

11. Hughes, *Winter Pollen*, pp. 118–19; see also Ian Robinson, 'Prose and Dissociation'; and Curtius, *European Literature and the Latin Middle Ages*, p. 266.

12. Hughes, *Winter Pollen*, pp. 369–72.

13. Hughes, *Winter Pollen*, p. 357.

14. Hughes, *Winter Pollen*, p. 349. Both American and French *vers libre* derived from Walt Whitman, *Leaves of Grass* (1855).

15. Eliot, 'Reflections on Vers Libre', *Selected Prose*, p. 36.
16. Eliot, *Varieties of Metaphysical Poetry*, p. 183.
17. Eliot, *Varieties of Metaphysical Poetry*, p. 202.
18. Clark, *Samuel Johnson*, p. 29.
19. Arthur Humphreys, 'The Social Setting', p. 36.
20. Clark, *Samuel Johnson*, p. 35.
21. Clark, *Samuel Johnson*, p. 16.
22. Clark, *Samuel Johnson*, pp. 33–4.
23. Clark, *Samuel Johnson*, p. 24.
24. Stern, *Rise of Romantic Hellenism*, p. 11, quoted in Clark, *Samuel Johnson*, p. 251 n. 37.
25. Clark, *Samuel Johnson*, pp. 1–2. Also Curtius, *European Literature and the Latin Middle Ages*, p. 32: '"Romance" is the name that the early Middle Ages itself gave to the new Latin vernaculars, precisely in contrast to the language of the learned, Latin... In Old French, *romaunt, roman*, means the "courtly romance in verse", literally "popular book"... In English and German eighteenth-century usage, "romantic" still means something "that could happen in a romance"'.
26. Edward Norman, *The Roman Catholic Church*, p. 17.
27. Clark, *Samuel Johnson*, p. 245.

Chapter 6

Romanticism

Romanticism is the underlying condition of literature and the other arts in a modern society. In such a society the dominant metaphysics is that of the religion of individual conscience, the result of Cartesianism and Lutheranism, which result in the politics of liberty and human rights: Voltaire, Rousseau, and the Founding Fathers. The religion of the individual conscience is the freedom to believe whatever you want and to do anything you want, so long as it doesn't harm others. In practice this means belief in anything and everything: from health to wealth to well-being; from stars to stones to spirits; from self to other to society; from nothing in particular to nothing at all. As we have seen, without conversion to another religion, however, these are but an extreme form of Protestantism, glorifying elements either of the historic tradition or of particular heresies associated with it. The attempt to establish a pure materialism or rationalism is subverted by the innate religious tendencies of human nature. Materialism becomes a religion, and rationalism becomes the means by which paganism is reintroduced, when Christianity is lost.

But this rebirth of paganism does not mean the rebirth of the tradition, for tradition has become identified with the Latin Classical tradition: while Paganism and Protestantism are identified with Romanticism. It is not therefore metaphysics but psychology that is incarnate in literature and the other arts. It is sceptical of the existence and so the authority of anything outside one's own mind: but it becomes self-defeating, it deconstructs itself. The logical conclusion of this is postmodernism, scepticism about the Enlightenment itself, the ability of reason to provide access to truth. The consequence is the solipsism and existentialism of Beckett, Sartre, Camus or Houellebecq, and the nihilism of the destruction of literature in English. But 'Romanticism was less a reaction to the enlightenment than an attitude concealed within it'.[1] It is a realignment of values so that art rather than the divine is the starting place of the quest for knowledge. Kant even derived his theology from his aesthetics, 'using aesthetic judgement as the proof of God'.[2]

The consequence for cultural values is that the individual artist or individual taste becomes sovereign: *de gustbius non est disputandem*. Authority is gained through popularity, the accumulation of individual preferences. This is a denial of the external authority of a religious, literary or artistic tradition, a discipline, to be aspired to, absorbed and learned. It is the denial of memory and of identity. In literature, in the West, that tradition is the Latin Classical tradition. Its literary standards are those arising in the ancient world, transmitted through the medieval ecclesiastical culture, and reborn through the Renaissance into the vernacular. The tension between the innate qualities and values of the vernacular tradition and language and the central Latin Classical tradition replicates the tension between tradition and the individual: between Rome and barbarism, between Catholic authority and Protestant dissent, between the authority of the Papacy and that of the individual conscience.

As a metaphysical principle is incarnated in culture, in literary form, the incarnation of orthodox Christianity is Latin Classical, and its rejection, the rejection of spiritual and cultural external authority, is secular and romantic. This gives rise not only to the varieties and distinguishing characteristics of the modern European literatures but also to varieties and degrees of relative classicism and roman-ticism. The modern movements in literature that we describe in these chapters are just this: the alternating attempts in literature to embrace or resist, to give in to or to hold back from this new culture, this new religion and this new society. For the new culture tends to reinforce the centrifugal and deny the centripetal, as the consequence of its individualism, its denial of external authority. The Romantic poets and novelists of the nineteenth century embody it in its purest literary form. That denial of external authority, that denial of the Latin Classical tradition, becomes in them an elevation of the vernacular and, in so far as it is classical, Romantic Hellenism.

Rhetoric was the primary literary technique of the Latin Classical tradition. Priority was given to the assimilation or reinvention of pre-existing materials so that it was impersonal rather than a cult of personality, an anonymous or collective endeavour, rather than a series of individual geniuses. As Curtius puts it, 'The majority of lyric themes, which the modern poet "creates" out of his own "experience" ... were material for rhetorical exercises'.[3] This, as C. H. Sisson says, 'comes to demolish the notion of expression'.[4] The age of Shakespeare was the 'outcome and flowerage' of this tradition: his reuse of old material, the rhetorical mode of representation of it and his personal anonymity, making him as much a part of that tradition as Chaucer or Dante were. 'The world of miracles and marvels is still alive in Shakespeare's last plays.'[5] The change, as we have seen, was to come soon after. Shakespeare himself embodied this crisis, the birth of the modern sceptical, subjective world, within his medieval heart. He was restrained and controlled by religious assumptions and belief: and belief was a very different thing then from what it is now. The religion of the individual conscience is a denial of external authority or discipline about belief: about what one should believe, and therefore what one should do. The only creed that is indisputable is itself.

It is the one thing that is not subjective or relative, the one thing that is believed with a religious intensity. This is unsustainable, there is no limit to scepticism, and the realization of this is what lies behind the crisis of postmodernism. The denial of the cultural authority of the Latin Classical tradition associated with historic Christianity becomes the denial of the authority of *any* external artistic and moral standards, that is, beyond apparent authenticity and power of expression: beyond the 'personality which makes it plausible'. And the 'personality thus expressed... [tends] naturally to be the unregenerate personality'.[6] The principal modern phenomenon is that of the expression of individuality, personality and identity, through innovation or originality, unrestrained by tradition or discipline. It is limited only by what people will buy, what is popular, what one can 'get away with', by how far one can go without infringing the rights of another sovereign subject to their own private dreams, there being no collective or public dream, beyond accumulation and mediation.

The intellect thus becomes an incidental element, contributing only to the maintenance of literary form, such as prosody and style: the vehicle for the expression of emotion, rather than the intellectual control, restraint or discipline of that emotion or content. The sense of struggle and moral value is lost, unless it is to be in touch with a 'deeper' or more 'authentic' self, rather than a less evil one, or one encountered through renunciation and reconstruction. It is also the denial of restraint, which is the stylistic essence of the classical tradition, and the essence of the pursuit of any artistic discipline. The consequence of this liberation is excess, and when feeling is unrestrained or uncontrolled, it becomes an intellectual excess. It may be an excess in any direction, of idleness or work, for example, or the contemporary excess of humanism over religion. It may be an excess of faith in reason, but may also be an excess of devotion, or religious emotion as it is an excess of scepticism, an excess of uncritical faith or religious emotion.[7] Eliot described the currents of Romanticism in the nineteenth century as deriving from Rousseau, 'escape from the world of fact, and devotion to brute fact... vague emotionality and the apotheosis of science (realism)'.[8]

Meanwhile the romantic desire for escape is the result of the replacement of the religious belief in transcendence by an artistic or political one. The consequence is the creation of the artistic idyll, the sanctification of nature as a contrast to the new urban industrial reality of life, or the creation of personal myths and cults which are in the end mere poetic fantasies. Romanticism thus retains a good deal of the spirit of their medieval origins, the Arthurian and other early vernacular literature, such as *Beowulf.* Romance language and literature was, at least in its origins, outside and distinct from the control and authority of the Church, whose culture was built upon the classics. Thus art itself becomes a religion. The artistic process, the individual creative personality or experience, and the fruit of artistic creation become versions of this sacred and liberated individuality. Art becomes the end rather than the means, the substance rather than the communication of a religion: the medium becomes the message, a sanctification of the imagination. The artist's efforts to make sense of the world become individual cults. We see this in poetry from Blake and Wordsworth to Hardy, Lawrence and Yeats; and it is the counterpart of the occult interpretation of Virgil in the Middle Ages. Poetic, literary or artistic emotion, and its expression, are no longer controlled, directed or restrained by an external intellectual or spiritual discipline or tradition.

The religion of the individual conscience is also thus the culture of the authority of personal feeling, whose defining characteristics are excess and escape, and the sentimentality that aggrandizes and glorifies the self, without the need for struggle. When feeling becomes reified and liberated from the control of an external spiritual authority the result is sentimentality and the aggrandisement of the personality of the artist. It is no longer controlled by an external or formal system, a system of living designed to integrate and maintain proportion between the mind, the emotions, the body and the spirit. For this to happen, a person must see their previous or natural way, not just of thinking but also of feeling and therefore of acting, as having had something wrong with it. They must in other words have an idea like that of Original Sin and the belief in it. And this is not just an intellectual but a behavioural and, most important of all, an emotional conversion.

Classicism and its variant Modernism thus become a call to the discipline of the emotions by the intellect, to restrain the excesses of and escape into emotion in Romanticism. It becomes a call to balance the rejection of tradition which undermines the Romantic project. It becomes a matter of artistic qualities and values rather than language or imitation. Many philosophies and beliefs abound in the liberal marketplace of ideas in modern societies, but most do not involve this reformation or reconstruction of one's attitude to one's own emotions, and indeed of one's own self. Most restrain emotion according to its effect on others, or one's own psychological or physical but not spiritual health. An assessment of which may be intellectual, but not according to any intellectual code, tradition or system which challenges those emotions. Its essence is the avoidance of the discipline of emotion, which is an 'escape from emotion' as it is an 'escape from personality'.[9]

The literary expression of emotion may be disciplined by a classical tradition or formal requirements, which, as with Neoclassicism, may be somewhat superficial. While those poets from Dryden to Johnson believed in their religion and were committed to the classical tradition, we have seen the limitation of their poetic range by comparison with that of the Elizabethans and Metaphysicals. Whatever poetic emotion or sensibility existed in their poetry was either borrowed from the ancients or associated with public political battles, rather than their consequences for private feeling, when, as we saw with Dante and Chaucer, emotion and its literary expression had been disciplined both by the literary techniques of rhetoric and the comprehensiveness of religion. We also saw that Shakespeare's lifetime had contained the battle between this and the ideology that would supersede it: the public battles of doctrine were also battles of private conscience and feeling. When it was superseded, by Puritanism, scepticism and the individual conscience, the discipline of emotion and its expression became personal and relative: a matter of private taste not of public doctrine.

Adherence to the Latin Classical tradition requires adherence to the emotional and intellectual discipline that sustains it. The practice of an art is itself a discipline; which is contained within the tradition. When all is made new with no regard for that tradition, the consequence is chaos: an empire of the perpetual present moment. The Romantics thus had neither emotional restraint nor intellectual discipline. What they did have was a deposit of poetic form and a new world of liberated feeling. It was this that gave their activities a continuity with the tradition, which is now lost. In the case of the novel however, the literary form was also new. In 'Reading and Writing' V. S. Naipaul speaks of the changing nature of literary forms, with the novel as an achievement and reflection of a particular period, supplanted perhaps by the 'first fifty years of the glorious cinema'.[10]

In an essay on Joseph Conrad, Naipaul says the 'novel as a form no longer carries conviction', non-fiction seems to be preferred.[11] Yet, this period in literature still forms our idea of ourselves, in particular of the decay of faith and its relationship to industrialization. This may be propaganda, wishful thinking, or self-fulfilling prophecy. The form of the novel and the new liberated feeling that was captured in Romantic poetry emerged at the same time as the new physical and social environment that was brought about by industrialization, and it was natural to connect them. The Romantic reaction was to run: either into the countryside, to commune with nature in a kind of neo-paganism, or into a dream world of the imagination. Neither was to engage with the new reality, but rather to allow the new world of feeling to run riot and to create a fantasy of escape from it or, in the case of the realist novelists, escape within it.

It was the beginning of middle-class flight from the city to the suburbs or the countryside, and into mental separation from the reality of the world around them. This began with Wordsworth's Lakeland cottagers and became part of the pre-

Raphaelite dream, put into practice by William Morris and others, and recreated ironically by the Bloomsbury set. This was in part a flight from the relativism of the new world of the cities to the nostalgic fantasy of recreating the certainties of the old world that had existed in the countryside: of recovering 'ontologism' or Thomistic or Classical realism, in the places where they had once formed the basis of life. But that was all long gone: the only place it remained were the few ecclesiastical institutions that were in communion, in fact or in spirit, with the Papacy. But that was the last thing they wanted, the city churches and cathedrals, the places where this spirit has been most persistent.

Blake, Wordsworth and Coleridge were thus the originators of the modern 'alternative lifestyle': of 'hippies' and the 'new age'. This mental separation was ideological as well as imaginative or physical. They thought that by an imaginative or ideological solidarity with the poor they could assuage their guilt at the difference in material circumstances. In doing so they developed a sentimental or unreal idea of poverty rather than one which engaged with it in a practical way, in service and redemption. They developed beliefs which satisfied their own consciences, which saved themselves first, rather than displaying a true concern for their neighbour. This became therefore a political reaction, a romantic revolutionary politics, believing in (but forever delaying) utopia, 'heaven on earth'. This utilitarian materialist attitude has been responsible for the worst atrocities in human history.

This is the metaphysical background to the movement, its incarnation in traditional verse forms and the new form of the novel. Indeed the very name novel suggests something new, originality, which Naipaul insists on. In the Latin Classical tradition, the individual is considered to be representing existing material, using rhetorical skills, and the idea of the individual creator does not exist. He must always be different, must present things already known in a different and graceful and accessible way, but the modern cult of originality is the cult of personality, of transcendence through the individual self and it is Romantic. There were several phases and types of Romanticism in poetry and the novel, the conventional history and criticism of which is familiar, while the history of literature and religious opinion in this and later periods is described in detail by Cowling.

In poetry, however, we may discern two traditions; the more Puritanical and introvert 'English Line', from Milton and Wordsworth to Hardy and Larkin, with their refusal to indulge language or image, their expression of pure mind or emotion. The other is a more extrovert, sensual, 'Catholic' or mythological reaction to this from Blake to Shelley, Keats, Browning and Yeats.[12] Blake is the progenitor of one type of English poetic Romanticism, Wordsworth of the other. Both are the consequence of the Puritan severance. One is open to the continued existence of a spiritual dimension and interested in it. The other denies it and mourns it in a melancholy and nostalgia that cannot employ the poetic resources or 'common myth-kitty'[13] that remains open to the other, albeit severed by disbelief. Neither denies the Puritan severance itself that is open to a Catholic renunciation which we shall see illustrated in the Caribbean in the last chapter. One is English, insular, introvert; the other is open, international. There is a strain of mystical romantic patriotism in each, whether the mythological version of Blake or the pagan nature-worship of Wordsworth, which was in truth a worship of his own creativity.[14]

Each derives from Milton, which Eliot regarded as having the 'historical thinness' of Puritan mythology, while Blake displayed, 'a certain meanness of culture. They illustrate the crankiness, the eccentricity, which frequently affects writers outside of the Latin traditions'.[15] This is exactly what we find in the novel, with its theological background of Protestantism and a rejection of continental cultural influences. The Gothic, Romantic, sensational and sentimental novel in the eighteenth, nineteenth and twentieth centuries is, as Naipaul describes it, mostly commercial writing.[16] It is disengaged from the Latin Classical tradition, as much as the Puritan and Protestant theology that lies behind it is disengaged from ecclesiastical Christianity. We see it, for instance, in Jane Austen's attempted resistance to sentimentality, the Brontës' puritan Gothic romances, Hardy's novels of pagan doom, to Dickens's London as symbolic of the corruption of the modern or fallen world's soul, which became Dostoevsky's model. The latter achieved a degree of cultural and theological maturity unavailable to the former, probably because of his formative experiences of real revolutionary activity and the harsh realities of life in a Siberian prison camp.

The real resistance is the defence of religious orthodoxy rather than artistic practices. As all modern art is romantic, the best that can be hoped for by those who reject it is to assert or project the existence of an alternative. That is the point of the study of literary or artistic history. This has occurred alongside a process where the representatives of the Christian religion, in particular in the Protestant churches, have come to see their purpose as the sanctification of the secular world they find themselves in. The religion of the individual conscience means modern people are able to find purpose and meaning in almost anything, from the mundane and everyday, to the lives of the rich and famous, and the stars and the cosmos. Christian ministers find challenging this difficult, and try to present Jesus as a nice, caring friend and humanitarian, rather than as a living and eternal sacrifice for our sin.

In this they represent the final push of a secularizing society away from seriousness in both religion and culture. They cleared the path for a society in which these things are no longer important or even relevant. The intellectual stimulation of work, and education for work, appear to be satisfactory for many, which is a consequence of Puritanism. The spiritual rewards of personal achievement and materialism, and the cultural satisfactions of relaxing entertainment and escape create a breach within ourselves.

The Romantics were the originators of that breach, the barbarians at the gate. They and their successors destroyed the literary and religious traditions that had dominated Europe for two millennia, and were responsible for its greatest cultural achievements. They cleared the way for the creation of a new culture and society, without religion and without literature, without a creative culture whose achievements would bear comparison with those of the past.

This new culture includes aspects of the realism that remains the dominant mode in fiction and drama, for an excess of realism is itself romantic. It is excess in any direction, it is why secular humanism is in essence romantic, with its excessive denunciation of or scepticism about the claims of any religion, or about man's spiritual or religious faculty. As we see in the next chapter, the only way to assert the existence of this faculty was to offend it, as with the school of Baudelaire which developed after the Revolution in France. The revivification of sensibility was therefore that of the unregenerate natural self and expression was no longer constrained by classical or continental example. We may compare this with the reaction in France, which had maintained in part a Catholic culture. In England the culture had been Protestantized as a precursor to secularity, in France only the state had been secularized at the Revolution. There the reaction to Romanticism, which emanated from Germany as much as from England, was to assert the emptiness of this new world, the vacancy in the new materialism, and to assert the existence of spiritual values, by offending them. In England the spiritual effect of Romanticism also extended into the Church.

Tractarianism was the ecclesiastical response to the eighteenth century, the Enlightenment. It was thus the response to a confessional state which had been established in 1688 and ended in 1828 and had been Protestant and aristocratic, latitudinarian and liberal. It was therefore the ecclesiastical counterpart of Romanticism, and both were a response to the 'rationalism' of this period. That 'rationalism' meant Deism, Arianism and Socinianism, it meant latitudinarianism and the broad church mentality, but it also meant philosophy, political economy and history. It meant removing from the world its charm, the spiritual and the mysterious, in favour of the utilitarian, the useful and the material good. But Tractarianism went deeper, into the causes of the eighteenth century, and arrived, with Newman, at the idea that the Erastian reformation itself was the mistake.

Romanticism thought of itself as a reaction against Enlightenment, but was in fact the artistic incarnation of it, and the sensibility of the Tractarians could not avoid it either: for they were still a part of the Church of England. It was liable to fall into a sacred or Catholic or Anglo-Catholic version of Romanticism: sentimental, emotional or lachrymose, whose devotional origins were not English, whose sensibility was dissociated, and whose intellectual position was inconsistent. The shortcomings in sensibility derived from its intellectual inability to reconnect itself with the Latin Classical tradition, and this was because its version of ecclesiastical Christianity was disconnected.[17] This becomes the 'current of feeling that starts with Newman, and passes through Arnold, Ruskin, and Pater to Francis Thompson, Lionel Johnson, Aubrey Beardsley, and even in a degraded and popularised form to Oscar Wilde'.[18] And it goes back to Crashaw, the Metaphysical Poet who represented feeling, feminine, rather than intellectual or masculine Catholicism, undisciplined by intellect. He was influenced by Italian poetry, which was dominated by the Jesuits, and the Spanish Mystics, and so was open to other traditions than the Greco-Roman Latin Classical tradition. It is what we might describe therefore as a Catholic Romanticism: 'primarily a devotional, a fervent temperament... [with] more in common with Cardinal Newman than with Thomas Aquinas'.[19]

The Tractarians would soon realize the paradox of Anglo-Catholic authority, which made them in effect

Congregationalists within an often hostile church.[20] While they could extract a Catholic liturgy from Anglican heritage, they could not avoid the reformed doctrine of the Thirty-nine Articles and the Erastian ecclesiastical structure. And many of them did not want to, preferring to remain patriotic, insular, and to retain the place of the individual conscience at the heart of English Protestantism. A church cannot just imitate the democratic institutions around it, however: there must be a central core of doctrine and dogma and the institutional means of protecting it. As the institutional authority of the King in Parliament was replaced by an internal democratic structure so was the doctrinal authority of the Book of Common Prayer, itself an amalgam of Lutheran, Calvinist and historic medieval Catholic doctrine. Once Catholic emancipation had been achieved in 1828, Anglo-Catholicism, almost as it was being born, became a logical inconsistency: It was to take another hundred and fifty years or so before it became a practical one.[21]

This absence of doctrinal or spiritual authority is incarnated in the lack of authority external to the individual in both romantic and postmodern culture. One variant of Modernism and one of Romanticism was religious: but the Tractarians, like the Caroline Divines, lacked the essential element of the tradition they admired, authority. The theology of the only doctrinal statement was 'Wycliffite, Lutheran, Erastian and Calvinist'[22] although their liturgical and devotional practice was a performance of the outer forms of the Church which had a genuine ecclesiastical form of authority. The state religion of the period 1688 to 1829 was thus a continuation of the Commonwealth and the Tractarian establishment of Liberal Catholicism as the religion of the state church was Romantic.[23]

Meanwhile the syllabic, 'orthodox', Protestant tradition in prosody was about to face a decisive challenge: and the challenge was to derive from the nature of the poetic image, and music, rather than form. We have seen that Wyatt 'created something wholly fresh and original... mingling old forms and new voices. It is the English imagination itself which has worked this miracle of transmutation.'[24] His introductions, like those of Chaucer, were from French and Italian, rather than the later borrowings from the Classics. The Augustan neo-classical revival was based on Latin, while the Romantic was a rediscovery of Greek.[25] The subject matter and content changed, however, from imitation to the expression of emotion. This continued in prosodic form until it was destroyed by modernism, and the introduction of *vers libre* from Whitman in America and, later, France. Since then prosody has been more eclectic and personal. The period of Thomas Hardy's adult life from 1858 to 1928 was the culmination of the era of orthodox or accentual-syllabic poetry, as it was of Protestantism as the religion of England.[26]

Already Gerard Manley Hopkins was working, in private, for his order the Jesuits frowned on poetry. His only reader was his friend the poet laureate Robert Bridges, who published Hopkins work after his death. He was forging a new metre, but the content was of the romantic Catholic line which begins with Ignatius himself. He would combine a Wordsworthian revelation of God in nature with Catholic theology and a Spanish Mysticism: but his great contribution remained prosodic. For Hardy the Golden Treasury remained his 'primary poetic manual' and his ambition to write poetry good enough for inclusion. Already he could admit, however, that 'inexact rhymes and rhythms now and then are far more pleasing than correct ones', which foreshadows T. S. Eliot's remark that the 'the ghost of some simple metre should lurk behind the arras in even the 'freest' verse'.[27]

---

1. Roger Scruton, *An Intelligent Person's Guide to Modern Culture*, pp. 28–9.
2. Ibid., p. 48.
3. Curtius, *European Literature and the Latin Middle Ages*, p. 158.
4. C. H. Sisson, 'Is There a Church of England?', *The Avoidance of*

Literature, p. 213. 'Nothing pleased Curtius more than to subvert a naively romantic instance of literary interpretation, by demonstrating the dependence of the text to which it had been applied on rhetorical precepts' (Peter Godman, 'Epilogue', in Curtius, *European Literature and the Latin Middle Ages*, pp. 599–653, 647).

5. Ackroyd, *Albion*, pp. 123–6.

6. Cowling, *Religion and Public Doctrine*, vol. 1, pp. 112–13, from Eliot, *After Strange Gods*, p. 63.

7. See T.S. Eliot, 'Religion without Humanism'.

8. Ronald Schuchard, 'T. S. Eliot as an Extension Lecturer, 1916–1919', Part 1, *Review of English Studies*, ns 25 (May 1974), p. 165, cited Eliot, *Varieties of Metaphysical Poetry*, p. 220 n. 44.

9. 'Poetry is not a turning loose of emotion, but an escape from emotion; it is not the expression of personality, but an escape from personality' (Eliot, 'Tradition and the Individual Talent', *Selected Prose*, p. 43).

10. V. S. Naipaul, 'Reading and Writing' (1998), *Literary Occasions*, p. 31. Many new world writers such as Faulkner and Hemingway seem to have had their imaginations formed by the cinema.

11. V. S. Naipaul, 'Conrad's Darkness', *The Return of Eva Peron*, p. 217.

12. Cf. Powell-Ward, *English Line*.

13. Philip Larkin, 'Statement', *Required Writing*, p. 79.

14. Curtius, *Religion and Public Doctrine*, vol. 3, pp. 550–1. 'Hardy's effect was undoubtedly that of a pagan beacon in the doom-laden world of which Kipling's paganism was to supply a confirmation' (ibid., p. 553).

15. T. S. Eliot, *The Sacred Wood*, chapter on Blake: a 'framework of mythology and theology and philosophy is one of the reasons why Dante is a classic, and Blake only a poet of genius'.

16. Interview, *Financial Times* (21 August 2004).

17. Ackroyd, *Albion*, pp. 127–8.

18. Eliot, *Varieties of Metaphysical Poetry*, p. 162.

19. Eliot, *Varieties of Metaphysical Poetry*, p. 162.

20. Aidan Nichols, 'A Personal View of Anglican Uniatism', citing Sheridan Gilley, 'The Ecclesiology of the Oxford Movement: A Reconsideration', *Nova* 1.1 (1996).

21. Graham Leonard, Preface, in Aidan Nichols, *Panther and the Hind*, pp. xi–xii: The Rt Revd Graham Leonard, Bishop of London, was himself a convert to Rome at the time of the ordination of women, in 1993.

22. Nichols, *Panther and the Hind*, p. 37.

23. All Anglo-Catholicism may be in the end liberal and romantic unless, perhaps, it is explicitly Anglo-Papal. The unsatisfactory relationship with the Latin Classical tradition may only be restored by restoration of the link between literature and the Papacy, the living incarnation of religious and cultural authority in postmodernity.

24. Ackroyd, *Albion*, p. 210.

25. Eliot, 'Music of Poetry', Selected Prose, p. 109: 'influence of Latin upon the innovators Wyatt and Surrey'.

26. Dennis Taylor, *Hardy's Metres and Victorian Prosody*.

27. Eliot, 'Reflections on Vers Libre', *Selected Prose*, p. 34.

Chapter 7

Modernism

As romantic criticism and practice underlies modern literature, so modernist criticism and practice, in particular that of T. S. Eliot, underlies this chapter and indeed this entire book. Likewise, the attempt to erase his influence and what he stood for has dominated the period since his death in 1965. At that point the last phase of the cultural revolution that attempted to wipe the slate clean of all that had gone before it had begun in the West, as it was about to in China. Just as that was an attempt to dispose of Confucianism as the founding and eternal principle of that society, so, in the West, this was an attempt to do the same, with the last remnants of orthodox Christianity.

In fact what happened was that it destroyed the last remnants of respectability and decency as the vestiges of Protestantism. What it left was, on the one hand, orthodox ecclesiastical Christianity and, on the other, secularism. As we have seen, the Reformation, culminating in the Puritan Cultural Revolution, had already attempted to do the same with ecclesiastical Christianity. This last revolution was also the attempt to erase the last remnants of the Latin Classical tradition as the vehicle of literary standards. It was argued that this was irrelevant to the concerns of modern readers and writers, and so, indeed, it may be: but at the cost of the existence of anything identifiable as literature. This, therefore, is the context within which modern writers conduct their activities.

It is the cultural incarnation of the relativist metaphysics that lie behind the phenomenon, now known as post-modernism. It is the logical conclusion of the process that we have seen developing over several hundred years: the replacement of the culture of being by the culture of thought, 'ontologism' by 'psychologism', Thomism by Cartesianism, and the consequent dissolution of all authority external to the individual, whether philosophical, political, spiritual or aesthetic. This included the doomed attempt to recreate the Latin Classical tradition in English through translation and imitation of the classics. Political authority, as much as that of religious or cultural, is now that of the individual, albeit aggregated and protected by rights against the infringement of others. Unless, that is, one happens to be a Classicist or an ecclesiastical Christian. An authentic cultural resistance, a cultural incarnation of the spiritual resistance that is being led by the Vatican, has yet to be found.[1]

We shall consider some possible attempts to do so in poetry, by Ted Hughes, Geoffrey Hill and Philip Larkin among others. And we shall see what success they have had in resisting the dissolution of the idea of cultural authority that is necessary for literature to exist. It may be that all that is possible is that it will exist, as Cowling suggested, '[a]s dissent, a Jacobitism of the mind which can do little more than protest its conviction that the modern mind is corrupt'.[2] Postmodernism is the culture of resignation at the apparent impossibility of this attempt while Romanticism is the underlying condition of the arts in a post-Christian society. Modernism, meanwhile, is the attempt to continue the fine arts and literature into this new society, this new world, which has emerged: to enable them to survive in a new environment; to capture the new experience, using the traditional tools of paint on canvas, sculpture, narrative and literary technique; to continue the culture of belief into a culture of unbelief, in other words – much as the Church adopted the culture of the pagan world, and transformed it into the culture of the West. As Roger Scruton describes it,

> The modernist is the one who consciously re-shapes the medium, in order that *old* intentions can be entertained... the self-conscious attempt to be part of a tradition – even the concept of tradition itself – is a modern phenomenon ... Only a modernist is concerned to *situate* himself and his art in history...

The cultural agenda of Eliot's Modernism, which derives from French Symbolism, is the incarnation of a spiritual or metaphysical agenda. As Scruton continues, in 'Baudelaire we find the most important project of modernism: the attempt to revive the spirit by offending it'.[4] That this is not the case with all or even with most modernist art reveals, to that extent, that it is in fact the exact *opposite* of the agenda with which we are concerned: the challenge to the Enlightenment or Romantic view of art as a replacement for religion. It is also therefore a challenge to the modern mind, which prefers the belief that the material world is the only world, within which progress is possible, and beyond which all is superstition, propaganda and lies. And which, eschewing the authority of traditional religions, permits itself the wildest superstitions and supernatural fantasies: what Naipaul describes as a 'strange combination of high technological advance and very low intellectual development'.[5]

The assertion that the spiritual life has an independent existence beyond the confines of the world of art is thus a direct contradiction of the dominant Romantic view – which includes Scruton. His complaint is that the achievements of Romantic or Enlightenment art have not been continued, that they have been undermined by the very forces which brought them into being. His solution, however, is not to repudiate them. Scruton, as Cowling puts it, is unable to resist the idea that the Enlightenment is an 'irreversible end to Christianity's plausibility, and he defends Arnoldian high culture rather as religion's successor than because of its Christian residues'.[6] The cultural agenda which Eliot was pursuing was founded on a spiritual or metaphysical agenda, albeit one that Eliot took until his late thirties to realise and to implement in his personal life. Even then it was only to Anglo-Catholicism, with its residual Protestantism, that he felt able to commit himself to. These were the metaphysics that lay behind his poetry. He wanted, 'a literature which would be "unconsciously" Christian rather than "deliberately and defiantly" so',[7] just as he seemed to want a Christianity would act as 'something deeper than belief', a kind of 'behaviourism' in which men would act in an 'unconsciously Christian fashion' at the 'substratum of collective temperament'.[8]

Cowling concluded that Eliot in the final phase of his career, after the war, was resigned and depressed about the prospects for religion and culture, and well he might have been. Eliot's Modernism was an attempt to continue the traditions of art and literature from a world of orthodox belief into a world of unbelief. It was an attempt to overcome the Romantic problem, that the content of belief was to be replaced by a belief in a method of communication: the medium had become the message. And this was because the theological metaphor, derived from the Bible, of the artist as creator, had been translated from ontological to psychological terms: the individual talent or genius had become divine.[9] The Latin Classical tradition was just that, a tradition, in which the individual saw himself as participating in the work of a community united over time and space, rather than an individual Romantic 'genius'.

This is what lies behind the characteristic flaws of Romantic art, the cult of personality, technical mediocrity, metaphysical confusion, empty mysticism, and the attempt to create a religious aura without a religious content beyond the idea of art and creativity itself. The challenge was established through the reintroduction of tradition as external to the individual and commanding him: in technique, in clarity and in the rigid distinction between the practice of art from any religious content it might have. This is the source of Eliot's interest in Metaphysical Poetry, and its decline from Dante, through Donne, to Baudelaire: because of the 'disintegration of the intellect'.[10] And this is the source of his criticism of English poetry after the Civil War, that it was not capable of metaphysical poetry at all. A poetry that could engage with difficult ideas, and translate them into emotional, poetic images as Dante had done, and as Donne did albeit in a corrupted, rhetorical way.

What distinguished England from France therefore was that France was still capable of a tradition that was continuous with the world that had existed before the Revolution. This had been a more violent form of reformation and secularization than had taken place in England and America, but it was no less complete. Baudelaire's reaction, and that of his school, to the new world enabled a continuity to be established that did not exist in England. It was the inception of Modernism: which would take both spiritual and secular forms. The secular form was in the end indistinguishable from Romanticism: for while it might adopt some of the techniques of Modernism, it rejected the metaphysics – which were crucial. While modernism might have literary consequences and outcomes, without a re-engagement with the metaphysics, it was empty, a reincarnation of Romantic modernity. This is what we see in the merely technical modernism of W. H. Auden, Ted Hughes, Geoffrey Hill and even Philip Larkin.

After his conversion Eliot would take a firm line against those modernist allies with whom he had been involved and who did not understand the spiritual purpose of the movement.[11] For Eliot it had been a gradual journey from the American Unitarianism of his youth to the Anglo-Catholicism of his maturity. As early as the university extension lectures, or evening classes, that he gave in 1916, before *Prufrock* was published, Eliot appeared to have arrived at something like his final position, however. Classicism was 'essentially a belief in Original Sin – the necessity for austere discipline'. And that 'a classicist in art and literature will be therefore likely to adhere to a monarchical form of government, and to the Catholic Church'.[12] But in elucidating this position he was associating himself with it, not committing himself to it. The situation was more complicated than that. The movement to which he was attaching himself was led in England by T. E Hulme, but his mind had been prepared for it by Babbitt at Harvard and Maurras in Paris. Eliot had pursued the postgraduate study of philosophy in these places. However his 'pervasive and sometimes corrosive scepticism was not to be easily overcome'.[13]

This 'corrosive scepticism' was not just related to his study of philosophy, and his personality, but also to the familial Unitarianism.[14] This was a modern secular religion of practicality and optimism well suited to modern America, but with its origins in England. It acknowledged the moral superiority of Jesus but not his divinity. This is the default position of many in the modern West, in the church or without. But Eliot had a deeper ancestral heritage of Puritanism, of which Unitarianism was a lapsed, secularised form; 'drained of its theology',[15] just as the modern liberal tradition in England is a secular form of Puritanism. Indeed, his ancestors had been among the Pilgrim Fathers, from East Coker, near Yeovil in Somerset. They went on to form part of the early Bostonian Puritan Aristocracy, establishing a long and prominent line of preachers and members of the national elite. While Eliot was inspired by Catholic models, in culture and thought, and while he was attracted to it in principle, he was unwilling to submit to it in practice, 'he was not to enter the Roman communion – for one thing, it smacked of republicanism and the Boston Irish'.[16]

This is the context of his reluctance to identify the collapse of the Latin Classical tradition with Puritanism or to adhere to the Roman Catholic position. It is the reason for the emphasis he places on the Society of Jesus and Spanish Mysticism in his account of the 'disintegration of the intellect'. We should also see this in the context of English anti-Catholicism, which has declined at the same rate as Protestant religious observance.[17] When there was observance it was still easier to be an Anglican than a Catholic. The Church of England was also more or less the state Church of English literature, and he wrote in English not in French. The Puritan soul of his ancestors was reincarnated into a modern Anglo-Catholicism, even though he 'remained a Calvinist or perhaps even a Gnostic in Anglican clothing'.[18] His early and logical intellectual commitment to the

Catholic Church was attenuated into an Anglo-Catholicism in its final flourish.

There was an important exchange with John Middleton Murry in the twenties, the period leading up to Eliot's conversion. Murry had written that *The Wasteland* 'expresses a self-torturing and utter nihilism'. 'To order such an experience on classical principles' would require 'an act of violence, by joining the Catholic Church'.[19] In the *Criterion* in 1923, Eliot took on Murry, asserting that the difference between the Romanticism that Murry was defending and Classicism was that 'between the complete and the fragmentary, the adult and the immature, the orderly and the chaotic'. This depended on the willingness to accept external authority in aesthetic, moral, social, political and spiritual life: a distinction between Protestantism and Catholicism, Orthodoxy and Heterodoxy, external and internal authority.[20]

In Chapter 2 we saw how the Romanticism of the Society of Jesus and Spanish Mysticism was a Catholic version of the Protestant divorce from the Latin Classical tradition. As we have seen, Eliot rested responsibility for the development of 'psychologism from 'ontologism', the origins of the dissociation and disintegration, with St Ignatius and Romantic Spanish mysticism. It was this that lay behind both the Catholic response to the Reformation and English Metaphysical poetry. And it was not in the Greco-Roman classical tradition but rather the result of Oriental, exotic or exogenous influences.[21] Eliot thought that Roman Catholicism after the Renaissance was just as liable to error as was Anglicanism or Protestantism, but it is hard to see how this can still be true in current circumstances. The problems which Eliot and Pound had addressed together were literary, to do with the failure of literature to engage with the new realities of human life: Pound's solution remained secular.

Modernism in English poetry began with Imagism around 1910 and derived from the French Symbolists. Eliot described it as 'a theory about the use of material'.[22] Imagism was a logical development of Symbolism and had important connections with the conceit.[23] As Pound was to put it in *How to Read*, 'literature has to do with the clarity and vigour of "any and every" thought and opinion... with maintaining the very cleanliness of the tools, the health of the very matter of thought itself... [i.e.] words...' or, in other words, 'to purify the dialect of the tribe'.[24] It was an echo therefore of what Wordsworth and Coleridge were calling for in their demand for poetic diction that was closer to the common speech of the people of the day, in the Preface to *Lyrical Ballads*: with which they led the Romantic Movement in poetry.

Pound wanted to reduce literature to its essentials and work back from there to a new and purified creation. Literature was simply language charged with meaning. 'Great literature is simply language charged with meaning to the utmost possible degree'.[25] And, as Pound put it of Eliot, 'he has trained himself *and* modernized himself *on his own*',[26] while Pound had modernized Yeats. Eliot had however modelled himself on the French school of Charles Baudelaire, including the poets Jules Laforgue and Tristan Corbiere. And, when the world had changed even more than the world in Wordsworth and Coleridge's day, the results were even more radical. The updating of English literature, its re-invention was thus led by two Americans, whose principal poetic success was Anglo-Irish and whose inspiration was continental.

It is sometimes argued that this was the end of English poetry, and with it English literature, coinciding with the end of the nation's pre-eminence in the world.[27] The American takeover of the poetic agenda and leadership in literature occurred at around the same time as that in world affairs: and they took it from the French and English. What followed was what Poe had feared, and Baudelaire and his school had foretold. Baudelaire in his *Life of Poe* described the United States as 'a gaslit desert of barbarism', in which Poe's 'inner spiritual life as a poet, or even as a drunkard, was a constant struggle to escape from the influence of this hostile atmosphere', who 'amongst a people without aristocracy the cult of beauty can only be corrupted, diminished and die'.[28] The French and English have not yet found a response: the English Line was to flounder afterwards, with none of Betjeman, Larkin, Hughes nor Hill making a really major contribution. Literature since has been trying to answer the questions posed by Pound and Eliot, to which perhaps the only solution is the 'reconstruction of the soul'.[29]

Modernism is the attempt to avoid the distinctive problems of Romanticism, which derive from its inclination to run away from the new world rather than to engage with it, and to confuse art with the transcendence provided by religion. The First World War could not be run away from, and the battle has been ongoing ever since, as the struggle for authenticity and engagement. It is a continual questioning of how traditional art forms, including the Latin Classical tradition, can be continued in a new and changing environment. Without a living tradition the artist must define or discover, redefine or rediscover one for himself. And Eliot's search for a tradition, a context, which went beyond the romanticism latent in English poetry took him far beyond Pound's technical literary criticisms. It became a criticism of the whole of Western civilization since the Reformation: a religious criticism, and an attempt to situate himself, to recover a tradition.

The modernist correction of the failure to criticize Romanticism, that Matthew Arnold had complained of in the nineteenth century, enabled other perspectives to emerge. Modernism was the resistance to the same culture that Johnson had been resisting: the culture of encroaching de-Christianization, latitudinarianism, the undermining of religious and cultural authority, and the consequent destruction of the Latin Classical tradition. But the manner and method of its 'classical' resistance was different. In his poetry, Eliot deliberately contravened Johnson's criticism of the Metaphysicals. His aim was to restore the proper relationship between literature and religion, which had been undone by the attack on orthodox Christianity, but he had also to establish it in his own mind and personality, and even in his soul.

His resistance was to the 'dissociation of sensibility', of literature, or poetry, from thought, from philosophy or theology. His aim was to put each back in its proper place, the place in which it had been when religion was a living reality. He objected to the Romantic idea that poetry was to do with the emotions not the intellect; that reason was in some way opposed to it, that a poem was emotion encaged in verse. He saw poetry rather as an 'escape from emotion' and he sought to disentangle the confusion of religion, or mysticism, and poetry, which became entwined once it was disengaged from the mind. The ideas of the 'disintegration of the intellect' and the consequent 'dissociation of the sensibility' were an attempt to respond to the process of de-Christianization and the destruction of the Latin Classical tradition. And its sources were foreign: it was an attempt to reintegrate or reinvigorate English with European tradition, contemporary, medieval and ancient, in the way that it had been when the Latin Classical tradition was still alive.

While translation was still a defining English literary art Eliot and the Modernists looked at the vernacular in a different way. Eliot and Pound reconstituted the English canon by considering it in the wider context of European and World literature, restoring a cosmopolitanism it had lost. As Ackroyd puts it: the English imagination and sensibility were formed by 'collusion and collision with European exempla'.[30] But by reconstituting it did they destroy it? They sought classicism or orthodoxy, the Latin Classical tradition, in formal qualities and an attitude of mind, which came from abroad. Eliot's style came from Jules Laforgue and Tristan Corbiere, which was derived from that of Charles Baudelaire, who was inspired by Edgar Allen Poe: an American. Yet, while Eliot's poetic models remained French he became an Anglo-Catholic rather than a Roman Catholic.

120

He retained more of his ancestral Puritanism than was consistent with communion with Rome: and with it perhaps the inability to resist the 'dissociation of sensibility' the loss of the poetic soul that this entailed.[31] However, the modern movement had French and Italian roots for Eliot: his criticism was based on seeing European literature as a whole, with English as one branch of a family tree. There was some truth in the accusation that it was not English, though there were English members of the movement: T. E Hulme, Wyndham Lewis, Arthur Symons and the Anglo-Irish Yeats among them. That its prime movers were Americans does not make their criticisms invalid, but reveals that the English have not yet found a way to deal with them. Perhaps the dissociation of sensibility and the disintegration of the intellect may only be overcome by the 'reconstruction of the soul' that reunion with Rome would involve. Meanwhile, in the Caribbean there are remnants, shipwrecks one might say.

---

1. Radical Orthodoxy is an Anglo-Saxon attempt to utilize continental postmodernism to this end.
2. Cowling, *Religion and Public Doctrine*, vol. 1, p. 453;
3. Scruton, *Intelligent Person's Guide to Modern Culture*, pp. 71–2.
4. Eliot describes this project in his essay on Baudelaire, who 'perceived that what really matters is Sin and Redemption... that damnation itself is an immediate form of salvation – salvation from the ennui of modern life ... it is this that separates him from the modernist Protestantism of Byron and Shelley... So far as we are human, what we do must be either evil or good; so far as we do evil or good we are human; and it is better, in a paradoxical way, to do evil than to do nothing: at least, we exist' (Eliot, *Selected Prose*, p. 235–6).
5. *The Nation* (Thailand) (11 April 2004).
6. Cowling, *Religion and Public Doctrine*, vol. 3, p. 631.
7. Cowling, *Religion and Public Doctrine*, vol. 1, p. 111.
8. Cowling, *Religion and Public Doctrine*, vol. 1, p. 120. Pope Benedict XVI describes how even in the Middle Ages 'there was the great mass of nominal believers and a relatively small number of people who really entered into the inner movement of belief'. This is because of the essential invisibility of God, which means that belief is a 'second mode

of access to reality', beyond the senses, to the 'true reality' that makes us 'truly human' (Joseph Ratzinger, *Introduction to Christianity*, pp. 49–51).

9. Curtius, *European Literature and the Latin Middle Ages*, p. 397. Also see Conclusion, below, for the way in which this is transmuted in a media culture into a more immediate divinization or cult of personality

10. Eliot, *Varieties of Metaphysical Poetry*, pp. 223, 227.

11. Cowling, *Religion and Public Doctrine*, vol. 1, pp. 118–19.

12. Ackroyd, *T. S. Eliot*, p. 75.

13. Ackroyd, *T. S. Eliot*, p. 76.

14. Ackroyd, *T. S. Eliot*, p. 16. The dominant influence on his immediate family was his grandfather, William Greenleaf Eliot, who founded the first Unitarian Church west of the Mississippi.

15. Ackroyd, *T. S. Eliot*, p. 17.

16. Ackroyd, *T. S. Eliot*, p. 159.

17. Norman, *Roman Catholicism*, p. 126.

18. Ackroyd, *T. S. Eliot*, pp. 169–70.

19. Eliot, *Varieties of Metaphysical Poetry,* p. 75 n. 29.

20. T. S. Eliot, 'The Function of Criticism' (1923), *Selected Prose*, pp. 68–71.

21. Eliot, *Varieties of Metaphysical Poetry*, pp. 75–6.

22. Eliot, 'Vers Libre', *Selected Prose*, p. 32.

23. T. E. Hulme, the leading English Imagist, who was killed in the Great War, had traced the problems of Romanticism, 'back to the individualism of the Renaissance' (Chris Baldick, *Criticism and Literary Theory,* p. 70).

24. '"Donner un sens plus pur aux mots de la tribu", Mallarmé said of Poe; and this purification of language is not so much a progress as it is a perpetual return to the real' (Eliot, *Varieties of Metaphysical Poetry*, pp. 289–90 n.: line 6 of Mallarmé's 'Le Tombeau de Edgar Poe' [1877], a line which Eliot was to adapt in translation for Part II of *Little Gidding* – 'To purify the dialect of the tribe' [194]).

25. Ezra Pound, *ABC of Reading*, p. 28.

26. Carpenter, *A Serious Character*, p. 258.

27. By, for instance, Philip Larkin and Auberon Waugh, the latter in his editorials in the *Literary Review*; also Donald Davie, *With the Grain*; and Powell-Ward, *English Line*.

28. Charles-Pierre Baudelaire, *Selected Writings on Art and Literature*, p. 163. Poe believed that 'amongst a people without aristocracy the cult of beauty can only be corrupted, diminished and die' (166).

29. Cowling, *Religion and Public Doctrine*, vol. 3, p. 697.

30. Ackroyd, *Albion*, p. 129.

31. Ackroyd, *Albion*, pp. 127–8.

Chapter 8

Postmodernism

Traditional Religions have in the past formed one piece with the cultures of the people who practised them. Among these peoples the same word was often used for religion, custom and culture. These forces and values held their societies together... It is to be noted that in Latin America the descendants of the people brought over as slaves from Africa in the sixteenth and seventeenth centuries have not lost everything of the religion and culture of their ancestors. Within the great variety of Afro-American cults, there are some that have kept very near to their original forms, such as Candomblé in Bahia (Brazil) and others that are rather syncretistic, as can be found in Haiti, Cuba and Jamaica... The Church respects the religions and cultures of peoples, and, in its encounter with them, wishes to preserve everything that is noble, true and good in their religions and cultures... Evangelization does not destroy your values but is incarnated in them; it consolidates and strengthens them.

(John Paul II, Address to Afro-Americans,
Santo Domingo, 12 October 1992)

Modernism was similar to Neoclassicism in that it was an attempt to resist the underlying Romanticism of modernity which had come to fruition. Whereas Neoclassicism had tried to do this by recreating the Latin Classical tradition in English, Modernism did so by questioning both the literary practices of Romanticism and the underlying spiritual developments that had given rise to it. However, Eliot was only prepared to go so far in his rejection of those spiritual developments. In particular, he was not prepared to transcend the Erastian Act of State that was the essence of the English Reformation. This may have been because he wished to continue to work within the confines of the Anglican tradition, which had contained most of English literature until the nineteenth century, and because he identified it as the only orthodoxy possible in England during his lifetime.

However, things have moved on since then. That literature has ceased to exist. And it is no longer possible to contain an orthodox ecclesiastical Christianity within the Anglican tradition.[1] In post-Anglican England it is necessary therefore to take the further step of questioning the entire culture that resulted in and from the Reformation and the development of Cartesianism. In this way a fuller understanding of the entire European cultural tradition associated with ecclesiastical Christianity may emerge, the Latin Classical tradition, and with it a way of resisting the cultural and metaphysical nihilism of postmodernity. This is a development of the opposing element of Modernism to the one we have described, the attempt to create a secular religion to replace the romanticism that was the consequence of liberalism: Marxism. This became an intellectual force at the same time as Modernism attempted its reactionary reconstruction, and by the thirties was the secular religion of a number of writers, including Auden. After the Second World War it would return in the English theatre, in Pinter, Brenton and Shaffer, for example.

The development of postmodernism was a development of Marxism, and other post-Hegelian philosophies, which included existentialism: a kind of liberalism without faith in reason and order. This was to take over the entire culture of the West, when faith in reason and liberal progress was lost, and all that was left was feeling. This became the sentimental humanism which is the inspiration for contemporary literature, culture and politics. It does not attempt intellectual engagement with itself or to understand its historical genesis, antecedents or heritage. It is existentialist, solipsistic, narcissistic, childish and self-indulgent. It sees no reason to engage with the high culture of the past because it feels that it has been liberated from such 'judgemental' or 'oppressive' phenomena, and indeed it has. As a culture it is childish also in that it is very young, and is unlikely to mature until it begins to develop self-consciousness about its own genesis.

Romanticism was in part a rejection of Neoclassicism and in part a continuation of it: it was also 'a reorientation within a surviving classical tradition from a Roman to a Greek Axis'.[2] But there is a further unity to these movements, and their successors, Modernism and postmodernism: disunity. They are different aspects of a single movement or phenomenon: the culture of secular, liberal, materialist modernity. And Romanticism is its purest incarnation, the 'emphasis on feeling, individuality, and passion rather than classical form and order'.[3] Modernism and Neoclassicism were thus a product of the same kind of Jacobitism or non-Juring sensibility. But while they may be reactions or resistance to modernity, they are its children nonetheless: and modernity is, as we have seen, the child of the Reformation. In particular it is the child of the 'psychologism' we saw incarnate in those theological forces on either side, the Puritans and the Jesuits. Postmodernism is also the consummation or the logical conclusion of this cycle: for it denotes nothing, or nothingness, the absence of pattern or movements, or principles, or even literature or a creative high culture itself.

It is modernity without the remnants of the Latin Classical culture, without a literature which maintains standards between ancient and modern. It is the logical conclusion of the development of the authority of the individual, the establishment of the 'dictatorship of relativism which does not recognize anything as for certain and which has as its highest goal one's own ego and one's own desires'.[4] It is solipsism and existentialism, the denial of the possibility of communication or shared rationality. In this respect it is the consummation of Romanticism, the exaltation of personality and passion; a final denial of classical form and order, whether intellectual or stylistic; and the rejection of the possibility of a common endeavour or tradition. It is the context of this book, which considers the grounds upon which standards were erected before in order that those who might lament the absence of the fruits of such standards may see how to re-establish them.

The only possible grounds are, as we have seen, ecclesiastical Christianity and its cultural incarnation in the Latin Classical tradition. An egalitarian religion of human rights is a dictatorship of relativism, a denial of religious and cultural authority: and hence the death of literature. Each modern intellectual and cultural movement has come to prominence at a different historical moment, with different literary forms associated with it. Each to some extent represents a development out of the other, and a response to the historical moments of modernity itself. And their level of self-consciousness as movements has increased as they have progressed, with postmodernism as the movement to end all movements, the end of all movements, as it is of everything else. Now almost every word that is written is a manifesto, a statement, a theology or anti-theology, rather than an unselfconscious work of art, a contribution to the tradition or communal enterprise, as it was in the Latin Classical tradition. What concerns us here therefore is not so much what postmodern theory has to say about the relationship between religion and literature as the fact that there *is no* literature.

It often seems to think that it has replaced literature, and perhaps because of this, it does nothing to encourage it. Rather, it discourages the idea that literature or religion has any meaning. The ideas of literary standards or tradition or meaning are undermined as are the possibilities of religious truth or knowledge. All that remain are 'discourses' which disguise power. The French literary critical idea of 'discourse', which derives from Jacques Derrida, is related to the ancient rhetorical idea of discourse. Its purpose, however, is the opposite and is corrupted by the Marxist idea of all culture as 'ideology'. This is taken up in particular among postmodern dramatists, such Harold Pinter, who conceive their work in political terms, and thus as part of an ideology of resistance. This is the death of literature as an independent, integrated activity. At least in the work of his master Samuel Beckett its absences felt like loss. There remains the memory of the creative interplay of the Christian and the pagan, whereas the concerns of Pinter are purely worldly.

Postmodernism is thus the condition of modern society and culture, and in particular of literature, after the initial creativity of Modernism had waned around the time of the Second World War. This is also the time in which Christianity underwent its final removal from its position as the underlying or default religion, belief or ideology in the West. It has been replaced by an ideology or religion which sees religious matters as private or irrelevant, with no business interfering with the public process of aggregating individual interests in a democratic liberal system. This period is perhaps more honest, where logical conclusions are reached and acted upon, but it is also thereby more empty. It suggests that overarching explanations and concepts such as reason and progress (the secular successor of providence) have become problematic, and that this is because of relativism.

It is not obvious that this says anything especially new or that it adds much to modernist ideas, and it is a matter of taste as to whether it is thought useful. The essence of postmodernism is this final achievement of relativism, although there is little new in it beyond the scepticism that was contained within Descartes and Luther. All it does is to apply this scepticism to the Cartesian Enlightenment itself, and the remaining orthodoxy of Lutheran Protestantism, and this is no more than the underlying intention of the original Romantics. 'Do not all charms fly / At the mere touch of cold philosophy?... Philosophy will clip an Angel's wings / Conquer all mysteries by rule and line / Empty the haunted air, and gnomed mine – / Unweave a rainbow'.[5] Keats's poem echoes Blake's portrayal of Newton: measuring but not experiencing the beauty of the universe.

But what remains when philosophy and the remnants of orthodox theology are emptied? The answer is the nothingness of relativism, but nature abhors a vacuum, and in this and the next chapter we see with what this emptiness is filled. 'When people stop believing in God they don't believe in nothing – they believe in anything.'[6] We already know that it is not literature or orthodox religion. The question it raises is whether the material and political gains of postmodern or postindustrial society are worth the intellectual, artistic and spiritual losses. In a democratic system the answer will always be 'yes', or an agglomeration of 'yes-es', but the question remains: what are the practical alternatives? The idea and ideas of postmodernism are not in themselves useful or constructive because their essence is negative. What it does, however, is to posit that the Modernist project in the arts and the Enlightenment project in general have run into difficulty.

This provides an opportunity to re-examine the foundations upon which the edifice of modernity, and its self-destruction, have been built.[7] Whether it would be possible to revert back to Romanticism or Neoclassicism is an open question, but one of the main ideas associated with postmodernism and literary theory is that movements such as these are over, that there are just individuals working without any overarching framework. The problem with which we are concerned in literature, however, is that individuals are *not* working: or that the work of those who are trying is damaged by the absence of the sense of working within a living literary tradition. What we are concerned with is why all this activity produces nothing like literature, or rather that it produces a lot that is *like* literature, but nothing that *is* it.

Some say that it is Modernism itself that is to blame: that it was international Modernism that destroyed the native English Romanticism at the beginning of the twentieth century.[8] But we have also seen that it is modernity that is the problem, its culture and belief has no use for anything but a personal private religion, without any authority to direct it beyond what the individual is willing to subscribe to on their own terms. And as the reason is religious, so the solution must also therefore be religious too. If the resistance or solution is the Latin Classical tradition associated with the Church, then it is as much for the church to realize this as the rest of the culture. But neither the Church of England nor Protestantism in general are capable of this reconversion, this re-establishment of grounds, for they are themselves the product and a part of this relativism, this 'psychologism', this 'corrosive scepticism'.

The post-Reformation vitality in English literature begins therefore to look like a doomed Protestant attempt to replace the Catholic culture that they had erased, which collapses once its logic is worked through to its democratic egalitarian relativist conclusions. However, while there is no literature here, there is vitality from elsewhere. The aspect of postmodernism that is described as postcolonialism is in fact a widespread movement of peoples which includes a cultural and economic colonization of Europe, and the rest of the world, by America. The creation of a multicultural society is the counterpart to the postcolonial creation of a globalized economy, which poses a challenge to the traditional cultures of each side and to the identity of individuals. The economic advantages of this are the conventional wisdom of politicians, but the cultural consequences are rarely discussed.

Mass immigration has been the counterpart to the decline of Protestantism in England, and the Romantic-Protestant form of English or British identity which accompanied imperialism, as lamented by Philip Larkin and Enoch Powell among others. The very presence of so many immigrants in England with their very different religions and cultures poses a fundamental challenge to this Romantic-Protestant worldview. It encourages the kind of meditation on a deeper understanding of English, European and indeed Christian identity which embraces the first thousand years of its history rather than just the last five hundred. As Ackroyd expounds at length, English culture and identity has 'always been a counterpoint of cosmopolitanism and introversion' founded on a secure religious identity. It is the absence of the latter which has made the post-Second World War period unusual: the demise of the Romantic-Protestant version of the Chosen People narrative and its replacement with a libertarian, relativist, neo-pagan individualism.

The historical decline of European imperialism after two world wars had sapped their vitality, coincides with the rise of so-called post-colonial literature. This process had developed further in the Spanish-speaking world than the English, because the bulk of that Empire had been lost by the time that the British Empire reached its zenith. The British had lost the American portion of it, however, before the movement for Latin American liberation took hold in the nineteenth century. These lost possessions provide a level of literary creativity which has been lost in the parent culture, now that English is spoken throughout the world, including as a lingua franca between foreigners. We began by considering two medieval writers, one from the Latin and one from the Anglo-Saxon world, Dante and Chaucer, both poets, the originators of a vernacular out of the Latin Classical tradition.

We now consider two such contemporary writers, perhaps the greatest in the English-speaking world and the greatest outside it, both writers of prose. As we concentrate on one aspect of their writing in particular, the beliefs, and especially the religious beliefs, that their writing incarnates, we see that as we are haunted by religion so we are haunted by literature, albeit by other people's religion and other people's literature. Gabriel Garcia Márquez is perhaps the most widely read and respected literary writer in any European language, whether in his native Spanish or in English translation. While perhaps the most respected literary writer in English, although not the most popular, is from the small island of Trinidad, off Venezuela, a few hundred miles along the Caribbean coast of South America from the small Columbian town of Aracataca where Garcia Márquez grew up.

'Ten weeks before he died, Mr. Mohun Biswas, a journalist of Sikkim Street, St James, Port of Spain was sacked.' The beginning of *A House for Mr. Biswas*, revealing the end of the story, as V. S. Naipaul begins his struggle to understand his inheritance from his father of the vocation of writer in English and his disinheritance from the Hinduism of his ancestors. It tells the story of a man's struggle to find a home: a search with echoes for us all in our globalized multi-cultural world, a search for identity which is in the end religious and cultural. It is a search which Naipaul explores in his parables of the mixed societies of Trinidad and the New World, England, Africa and India. He has made his physical home in England, his intellectual one in the European tradition of literary humanism, and his spiritual home in his commitment to the values of the American constitution.

Underlying it are sub-continental instincts that we might describe as a Gangetic secularism or paganism, which is reflected in his support for the Hindu nationalist party in India, the BJP. He says that 'idea of the pursuit of happiness is at the heart of the attractiveness of the civil-ization to so many outside it or on its periphery'.[9] Thus he shares the deism of the Founding Fathers, their rejection of revealed religion and the spiritual imperialism of the revealed religions, Islam and Christianity.[10] It is equally accommodating to the natural religions of Africa, India, and pre-Christian Europe, that were subject this imperialism, as it is to modern liberal relativism. He reveals his 'great feeling for the religions of the earth', suggesting that the 'missionary who wants to convert them all to a revealed religion is arrogant and destructive'.[11] This is in contrast to the self-understanding of the Catholic Church claims to respect the 'religions and cultures of peoples, and, in its encounter with them, wishes to preserve everything that is noble, true and good in their religions and cultures'.[12] This is called 'inculturation'.[13]

When pressed on his central moral beliefs he shows that the rejection of revelation is also the rejection of external moral authority. 'I believe in a kind of cumulative conscience of mankind. We all possess this conscience... knowing yourself. I feel that that gives you the place where you stand... the moral centre... '[14] This is the same reason and conscience which is found in all natural religion or paganism, which revelation transcends. However, while his commitment is to the dominant cultural mode, Naipaul is a stern critic of the recession of literature, as we have seen. While this dominant culture of 'knowing oneself' and the 'pursuit of happiness' may be able to survive without literature, the attack on spiritual imperialism is also an attack on the traditional English self-understanding of themselves as a 'Chosen People': a culture which Naipaul reveres and sees as a force for good'. Meanwhile, the triumph of liberal relativism and the undermining of imperial values may itself be a consequence of the end of empire and its subsequent implosion.

Through this process both the English language and its literature have become the glory of a much wider group of people, including Naipaul for whom his ancestors', 'migration, within the British Empire, from India to Trinidad had given me the English language as my own'. *In The Enigma of Arrival* Naipaul wrote that, as a recent arrival from the Crown Colony of Trinidad, in London in 1950 he 'was at the beginning of that great movement of peoples that was to take place in the second half of the twentieth century... a movement between all the continents'.[15]

The beginning of the book describes the narrator's Wordsworthian wanderings on Salisbury Plain, echoing the poet's youthful work. It then describes the replacement of the old society and culture by the new one Naipaul represents as the new arrival. It therefore continues the tradition and metaphor of the spiritual wandering of the creator, the search for a home, as well as the creation of the postcolonial or postmodern world. Naipaul describes how he took the title of his book from the title of a surrealist painting, and how he learned later that the titles of Chiroco's surrealist paintings had been given by Apollionaire, a poet who himself stood on the cusp of the symbolist movement in poetry and surrealism. Surrealism and its sister phenomenon Dada have a special relationship with both the Caribbean and the modern world. Their emergence is related to the 'discovery of the unconscious' while its originators, including André Breton, acknowledge the influence of the Caribbean way of looking at the world in its inception. It is also perhaps the decisive incarnation of contemporary belief in art.

Joseph Beuys was typical of postmodern artists in seeing his role as being that of a Shaman in a postmodern, postindustrial society, operating in the realm of the collective unconscious through his installations and events. We have seen how Ted Hughes, as a student of anthropology as well as English, saw his and other great poets' roles in a similar light. The most complete form and the consummation of the symbolic, the artistic, poetic or literary, way of seeing the world is the religious. There, texts and images have meanings beyond those that the human creators intended for them, meanings which go beyond and derive from elsewhere.

This Caribbean surrealist and unconscious way of looking at the world, taken up in psychology or anthropology, is a modern, secular incarnation of this religious phenomenon. It contrasts with the organized and disciplined, 'ontological' vision of the *Commedia*, or the mysticism of the Victorines, where the emotions and the imagination are disciplined by the intellect. It is not the ordered vision of medieval European mysticism, disciplined by dogma and intellect, not that perfect supernatural way of coming to terms with reality, religion itself, including the scepticism that is the husbandman of a disciplined faith. It is rather individualistic, irrational and undisciplined.

This is the first aspect in which the Caribbean, as symbol or as fact, is universal. It is the type of this contemporary culture, prefiguring and embodying it in microcosm, beginning and even in some respects causing this wider and now near-universal 'cultural-mixing'. And it is also key to the historical origins and development of capitalism.[16] It is a symbol and a metaphor for each, at once the beginning and the end, the origin and the outcome of the expansion of Europe, which has in turn created a new world and destroyed the values of old Europe. And it has done so in a way that the United States could not, for that society began its independence in clear imitation of Europe, and did not yet embody this mixing. The second respect in which it is important is that this cultural mixing has become in turn a mixing of beliefs. Garcia Márquez describes the Caribbean and Latin Americam origin of his style as 'Magical Realism': 'we consider so-called magical situations part of everyday life, like any other aspect of reality... I see myself as a realist, pure and simple'.[17]

Márquez attributes its local manifestation to 'myths brought over by the slaves, mixed in with Indian legends and Andalusian imagination', while he learnt it personally from his grandmother with 'her way of talking naturally about the supernatural world'.[18] This 'cultural mixing', of 'Western culture, the African presence, even some Oriental elements, all added to the native, pre-Columbian tradition', has produced a syncretism, a mixing of beliefs and perspectives, which is a religious version of the cultural mixing. Those oriental elements include, in Trinidad and elsewhere in the British West Indies, Naipaul's Indian patrimony. It is the incarnation of the religious confusion inherent in liberal modernity that is a consequence of the demise of external authority, including that of revealed religion. As we have seen, the modern secular or godless religions have not in fact progressed beyond belief in the supernatural, but rather they have discovered, invented and reinvented new forms of it.

In Márquez this superstition is obvious and inherent while in Naipaul it is more elusive, perhaps because Naipaul's version is more Anglo-Saxon, Protestant, even Brahmin. But while Garcia Márquez's contemporary incarnation of the Latin tradition may be more Catholic it is not thereby more classical. Both share the willingness to experiment, to write fiction and non-fiction, literary and journalistic prose, autobiography and historical reconstruction and to combine them all, thus reverting to the origins of the novel in the margins between biography, autobiography and history.

What this shows is that their roots in European tradition are not obscure, but that they have absorbed it and also learned the lessons of European Modernism. However, the tradition that they have perpetuated amid the experimentation is not one of an order restrained and disciplined by tradition and external authority but rather that of the free spiritual self-exploration and discovery that is the keynote of the modern culture that they exemplify.

Although Márquez does not write in English he says he prefers his own books in English translation. 'They're not better written or more poetic, but they have fewer words than I can achieve in Spanish... because Spanish is such a sinuous language.'[19] Compare this with Naipaul, who said in a 1973 interview with the journal *Caribbean Contact* that he thought Latin America 'a fifth-rate continent, largely because of the language and the cultural heritage... It's a second-rate [language], without any literature'.[20] Márquez's literary inspiration is also North American, albeit in the Southern Gothic of William Faulkner and the Hispanophile Hemingway: but his politics and worldview are not, or seem not to be. He says that American writers are 'the literary giants of the 20th century' and 'New York is the greatest phenomenon of our time', at the same time as defending Latin American Socialism against American Imperialism.[21]

However, while his life's work has often been a way of finding a voice for, mythologizing and perhaps anaesthetizing, the distress of the poor, for which he often blames the North, his support for the Latin American left leaves him close to progressive opinion north of the border. While Márquez's detachment is different from Naipaul's, both have their roots as writers in journalism and both are of the 'plantation' society. The main difference between the two may be, however, that Naipaul's secularism is more of the right and Garcia Márquez's of the left. This may also be why, when the writing of both of them is important to us, Garcia Márquez's is the more popular. Naipaul writes in the Protestant and empiricist tradition of the English-speaking world, which has become secular. Márquez writes in the Catholic Spanish tradition, which accommodates many other cultural and spiritual phenomena. The postmodern Western world lives between two spiritual tendencies represented or incarnated by the cities of Rome and Havana: spiritual order or superstitious relativism. This is a description from Juan Pedro Guttiérrez, a contemporary Cuban novelist.

> There was a knock on the door. I was surprised but pleased. There were two women with Bibles in their hands. They were preaching. They do that a lot in this satanic district. They go from door to door, but here we're all from Africa. So we practise *santeria*. When the preachers ask 'Do you believe in God ?', the usual reply is: 'Yes, but we have our own religion. And it's the true religion because my grandmother left me all this and...' The preachers make their excuses meekly, knock on the next door, and the same scene is repeated. And so on *ad infinitum*.[22]

Santeria is the syncretic religion of Cuba that was disguised by the official atheism. It derives from the practice of the religion of the Yoruba people of Nigeria, disguised as the worship of the Catholic saints, arising from the restrictions of slavery, which Cuba was the last to abolish. It is thus allied to the official doctrine by association with the rejection of imperialism, including contemporary economic and democratic imperialism. It incarnates the nation in its ethnic mix and its culture, where the official dominance of European modes disguises the reality of the pre-eminence of African modes of thought, worship and culture. And it thus incarnates the syncretism and disguised paganism that is the spiritual reality of the post-ecclesiastical West. It is incarnate in various post-literary cultures: including pseudo-rationalistic ones such as egalitarian socialism and scientism. Whether these beliefs are grounded in earlier traditions or in modern rationalist fantasies, they are all the same in that they are unexamined superstitions. The modern idea of progress for instance or of free-will can be seen as lapsed remnants of Christian doctrine.[23]

Each of these writers is of the Caribbean, with Havana as its symbolic capital, 'the Paris of the Caribbean' and its incarnation of our new world. We might perhaps therefore describe the Caribbean as incarnating the 'unconscious' of modernity, with its rejection of external spiritual authority. The difference may be that in the Caribbean the beliefs are genuine and traditional, whereas in the wider world this credulousness or superstition, this magical view of reality, is often accompanied by an exterior scepticism, cynicism or even nihilism. The Caribbean has been thus described, in the coded terms of contemporary literary criticism, as a 'cultural meta-archipelago' that proliferates endlessly around the whole of our postmodern culture.[24] And perhaps somehow it is, with Havana as its capital, representing the submerged paganism, the traditional beliefs and culture into which Christianity is incarnated, even in Europe, and which it sanctifies. Magical Realism is the mode not just of Latin America but of the whole of postmodernity.

It may represent indeed the paganism of the goddess, denied but converted into materialist form by Puritan rationality: that is also the paganism of literature, sanctified by the Church and incorporated into the Latin Classical tradition. As Márquez says, 'I believe many regions of the world are like this, full of wonder and mystery. Most people just don't see it.'[25] And we end with the lament of the only living writer of English whose achievements compare with those of the past. Naipaul describes the consequence of the incarnation in culture of the Anglican and post-Christian egalitarian religions of England as a deification of the demotic. 'To wish to become a writer is to have the idea of a civilisation, to take part in a high civilisation, as contrasted with life in that plantation society, and it has not worked out like that.'[26]

1. Because of Synodical Government, and because in the 1960s England shook off the respectability and decency that were the moral remnants of lapsed-Protestantism.
2. Clark, *Samuel Johnson*, p. 251.
3. *New Shorter Oxford Dictionary*.
4. Ratzinger, Joseph, 'Homily at the Mass for the Election of the Roman Pontiff' (18 April 2005).
5. John Keats, *Lamia*, ll. 229–37.
6. Attributed to G. K. Chesterton.
7. Again, this is what Radical Orthodoxy attempts in theology.
8. A position argued by Donald Davie in *Against the Grain*, Philip Larkin, and Auberon Waugh amongst others.
9. Naipaul, 'Our Universal Civilization'.
10. Naipaul, *Beyond Belief*, pp. 71–2.
11. Interview, *Literary Review* (August 2001).
12. John Paul II, address to Afro-Americans, Santo Domingo, 12 October 1992. Cf. Augustine: 'whatever was good, true or beautiful could be used in the service of the gospel'
13. See *Redemptoris missio* (1990) <http://www.vatican.va/edocs/ENG0219/_INDEX.HTM>,
   sections 52–4. <i>Incarnating the Gospel in Peoples' Culture <http://www.vatican.va/edocs/ENG0219/__P7.HTM>.
14. Interview, *Literary Review* (August 2001).
15. V. S. Naipaul, *The Enigma of Arrival*, p. 130.
16. Antonio Benítez-Rojo, *The Repeating Island*, builds on the work of Fernando Ortiz and Lydia Cabrera.
17. Interview, *UNESCO Courier* (October 1991).
18. *UNESCO Courier*.
19. *Los Angeles Times* (2 September 1990).
20. Raoul Panti, 'Portrait of an Artist', *Caribbean Contact* 1 (1973), pp. 15–19.
21. *New York Times* (7 April 1985).
22. Pedro Juan Gutiérrez, *The Insatiable Spider Man*, pp. 61–2.
23. Cf. John Gray, *Straw Dogs*.
24. Benítez-Rojo, *Repeating Island*, p. 9.
25. *Washington Post* (10 April 1994).
26. *Literary Review* (August 2001).

Conclusion

This book has argued that English literature has declined, almost to the point of non-existence. In this and previous chapters we examine what remains: the entrails, or shipwrecks, so to speak. It has argued that this decline has been concurrent with that of English Christianity, and it has examined the relationship between these two phenomena. The demise of medieval realist metaphysics and the rise of the modern thought culture have accompanied the demise of literature as the cultural incarnation of the central Latin Classical tradition of the West. The final phase of each has occurred since the Second World War with the final emergence of the new mass media culture. It might be said that now, in place of a religion of the book, we now have a religion of the mass media in which the cult of personality, of the individual, is consummated.

Time and death are transcended by the transmission and preservation of the image of the individual through television, film and sound recording, in a way they were not by literature or the other arts. Instead of the author's spirit, which is also the spirit of their times and tradition, what is recorded is the image of their body, speech and actions. It is a tele-visual religion, which elevates individuals, their identities, abilities or attributes, into a virtual pantheon of sub-deities. Those attributes elevated in the television culture include fertility or sexuality, health, physical prowess, strength, beauty, enterprise, wealth, imagination or emotion, all of which may be sublimated into a personal or collective belief-system or way of life. All are materialistic, none transcendent. Modern people 'believe in' sporting or political causes, business enterprises, products or brands, identities, secular charities, humanitarianism or human rights, in the same lukewarm, half-hearted or puritanical, angry, and self-righteous manner that they believe in anything.[1]

These individual or personal creeds or practices are built on political creeds or dogmas which sanctify principles of social organization such as equality or liberty. The intention is to work towards the creation of a heaven on earth, to build 'Jerusalem on England's green and pleasant land'. The idea of eternal life is redundant: death becomes something to be avoided and best forgotten rather than the fulfilment, meaning and purpose of life. However, while death retains its mystery, it remains, alongside suffering, as a primary source of spiritual questioning. And it does so even when religion is meliorative rather than eschatological, natural rather than revealed, 'world-immanent' rather than 'world-transcendent'. Rome and Havana, as we have seen, are its antitheses: the latter disguising its paganism with both Catholicism and an official Socialist Materialism and the former revealing spiritual order and historical continuity.

In the television culture the arts of the book have been replaced by the performance and personality-based arts of the new media. The word has been replaced by the image and, with it, the primary English and European tradition of high cultural achievement, literature, has been replaced by an obsession with the new media. It is this that attracts the young and talented, not poetry, or the other literary arts. If every generation has the same quantity of talent, of raw ability, the reasons for this literary decline must be cultural. The culture does not value the same achievements or cultivate the same virtues as before: there is just too much else to do now. And non-fiction is no substitute for works of the imagination, however good it may be: it is no substitute for 'fictions', whether in poetry or prose. 'There is too much television. The art of storytelling and character and all of that has been eaten away. You look at a country like France and literature there is finished.'[2]

After the Second World War, the only achievements were those of existentialism, expressing the nihilism, the literary nihilism, of the age. Such creative works are the memorial or monument to an age, a tribute to its civilization, and ours

140

will be an empty plinth. Our new mass media culture is a gaudy efflorescence of beliefs, motivations, lifestyles, habits and creatures of the imagination unleashed. It presents a scene reminiscent of the *Inferno*, Hieronymous Bosch or other works of the medieval or ancient imagination. A post-modern spectacle of the damned tormented by furies, a pantheon of the fallen, where the exalted fail to rise above it, except by excess. And yet, although 'the Enlightenment shattered the authority of the book and the Technological Age changed all the relations of life',[3] still the 'essence of technology is not something technological'.[4] These technological phenomena merely reveal the underlying situation, they incarnate its metaphysics: the lapse of Christianity and the emergence of a post-Christian culture.

It is a culture which has replaced God by man, Christ-ianity by secular humanism or neo-paganism, a culture of being by a culture of thought, ontologism by psychologism, and Thomistic or Classical realism by Cartesianism and an inevitable nihilism. Submission to external authority, whether in religion, culture, or politics, has been replaced by submission to the ego, to subjectivity, to relativism and the individual conscience, whether alone or aggregated by democracy. We have seen this develop as a theological and cultural phenomenon, but the final stage of the emergence of this culture has been political: the establishment of a rights culture, which legislates for the absolute primacy of the individual. It aggregates those individual preferences and choices through the development of the elective 'dictatorship of relativism': of a purer and purer, more absolutist democratic system. When the individual con-science is sovereign we inhabit a spiritual, moral and cultural anarchy, regulated only to the extent that it protects itself from others. And this fact that it has to protect itself from others is of profound significance.

The political incarnation of secular humanist values, in liberal democracy, is as much a theological and cultural as it is a political relativism. While much liberal thought has gone into the attempt to limit this relativism, to limit its absolutism, those attempts are inconsistent with its essence, which is individual choice, the individual conscience.[5] It is a logical and natural process which has led from medieval heresy, through Lutheranism and Calvinism, early Enlightenment ideas of high culture, philosophy and nobility, to the mass market culture of today. And yet, despite all this, the modern religion of the English may even now not be Liberalism, since it 'includes decency, respectability, mistrust of enthusiasm, an aversion to theory and an even greater aversion to the dogmatic expression of belief'. On this account, it is a 'low-keyed respectability which is the real religion of the English people'.[6]

While respectability and decency may have been the modern religion of the English until the 1950s, they were a remnant of protestant Christianity, with its peculiar moral tone. The cultural revolution of the 1960s saw the content of this morality, though not the tone, converted into the pieties and decencies of the new religion that has replaced Christianity as the state religion, with its political correct revision of respectability and its pagan consequences. This is the positive aspect, the indoctrination that accompanies liberal relativism, and it is unlikely that it can be avoided without an alternative belief-system, such as Roman Catholicism or, less reliably, Biblicist Protestantism. Without this the self-restraint that Christianity provided is lost: the external authority that controls the 'inner voice' of Original Sin, the unreconstructed will. The consequence of this is that the 'liberal state' has to employ more and more restrictive methods to control its supposedly freer and freer vassals.

We are reminded of Pope Benedict XVI's identification of Christianity with the tradition of liberty in Europe: without dualism, without an ultimate ethical authority which is outside the control of the state, in the Church, there is pagan totalitarianism. Without Christianity Liberalism becomes a self-defeating 'dictatorship of relativism'. The literary and artistic counterpart of this culture is Romanticism, in which the arts themselves, the act of writing or reading for instance, become religious, the source of transcendent purpose or meaning. It is a sanctification of the imagination and the individual creative act or experience, and this has a negative effect on both religion and the arts. Whereas Christianity provided an external discipline or control of the emotions and ego, romanticism exalts them, as does psychoanalysis and the cult of therapy and self-development, especially in its Freudian or theoretical form.[7]

The result of the dismissal of Christianity is the art of excess, whether in the direction of escape or fantasy, sentimentality, or of realism, which becomes morbidity and horror. It is the destruction of classical restraint, the discipline of formal artistic standards or a living tradition. The absence of this idea of standards, of comparison with the achievements of the past, the provision of an external, religious or moral, standard by which to judge a work of art, leads us into a 'dictatorship of relativism', of pagan subjectivity. The 'common pursuit of true judgement' or the 'approximation to an ideal order' dissolves into the mere expression of opinion, the articulation of taste.[8] And with it the motivation for achievement, for emulation of the achievements of the past, disappear as they merge into a 'provincialism of time', a perpetual present, in which shock and awe become the defining values of art, and the tele-visual culture is absolute.

The progenitors, therefore, are our spiritual leaders, the Christian leaders, the political philosophers and modern writers who have acquiesced and assisted in this corruption and decay. Whatever good intentions or high ideals they might have thought that they had, they did not have the intelligence, humility, restraint or respect for tradition, their spiritual and cultural inheritance, to understand anything beyond the hero-worship, personality cult and sovereignty of the self of the present day. Our literature is dead; it died with our faith. But with it died the popular anti-Catholicism which went alongside the patriotic Protestantism that was the creation of the English Reformation, an Erastian act of state, supported by sectional or class interests. Protestantism has been replaced as the religion of the confessional state by a dream of neutrality and secularity which doesn't know that it requires Christianity to exist, that it is a part of Christianity. Without it a more-or-less conscious positivism is inevitable and the less conscious it is the more pagan it is likely to be.[9] And it is unlikely that the Protestant churches will be able to survive or to retain their orthodoxy in a pagan secular relativist culture. This is the consequence of their conception of authority, which is vested in a book, or more vaguely in Anglicanism, in Scripture, tradition and reason. And a book (and tradition and reason) requires authoritative interpretation if it is not to become simply the expression of a private opinion, whether of an individual, or a group or of a nation. We are reminded that,

> Christianity became the religion of a book but, unlike Islam, it did not begin as such. The Pauline epistles are still earlier than the Gospels. Still earlier are the words of consecration of the Mass, which Paul 'delivers' to the Corinthians even as he had 'received' them (I Cor. 11:23ff.), and the creed (I Cor. 15:3ff.), which goes back to the original congregation at Jerusalem.[10]

Still the Lutheran dependence on the individual conscience, the absence of external authority, has become the essence of modern belief and undermined the medieval tradition of an integrated and holistic culture. But it is not the only alternative. For the question is not one of ecclesiology but of orthodoxy; and this has implications for art. The Church of England still has the Book of Common Prayer, but it does not use it.[11] But, is a doctrine which incorporates a Calvinist doctrine of the sacraments a sufficient basis for a Church to exist in the intellectual and social circumstances of modernity, or even at all?[12] Samuel Johnson who 'regarded religion as having an integral relation with literature'[13] believed that there was an essential agreement on doctrine between the different churches in his time, and that the differences were in fact political. 'Sir, I think all Christians, whether Papists or Protestants, agree in the essential articles, and that their differences are trivial, and rather political than religious.'[14]

This is no longer true, if it ever was, and the question becomes the one of which ecclesiastical or doctrinal structure is most able to resist the 'corrosive scepticism' and relativism of modernity and postmodernity. Contemporary English churches and in particular the state Church are little more than a means of sanctifying secular beliefs, values and prejudices, such as sexual equality, materialist humanitarianism and human rights. Most contemporary churchmen are more guided, influenced and directed by secular philosophy, theology and culture than that of historic Christianity.[15] They are about as far removed from orthodox or historic Christianity as the contemporary social structure is from the medieval. The orthodox position is sustained, articulated and represented almost alone by the independent ecclesiastical authority of the Papacy. That criticism stems from a conception of human nature that is expressed in its 'theology of the body' which derives from the sixth commandment. Is man a spiritual or just a physical being: as Disraeli put it, 'is man an ape or an angel'?[16] There is self-definition in answering this.

Contraception and marriage become the most central questions in this regard in everyday life, the other 'life' events being rarer occurrences. The collapse of matrimony in contemporary Britain, the apparent lifting of the stigma attached to illegitimacy, and the 'culture of death' that Pope John Paul II identified across the Western world show the extent to which Christianity has been jettisoned. Modern, post-Renaissance, English literature is the child of Protestantism, itself the child of printing, and the scientific culture that emerged out of the twelfth century. A medieval English religious particularism or gallicianism became

145

associated with the empiricism exemplified in the thirteenth and fourteenth centuries, respectively, by Roger Bacon and William of Ockham.[17] That this became Protestantism required the influence of continental doctrines and their suitability to the convenience of elites which rejected external authority on both a personal, class and national basis. The Puritan Cultural Revolution, with its combination of the religion of the individual conscience and its doctrine of the elect, was the decisive force that lay behind the emergence of liberalism, and was an elite imposition. As Puritanism has atrophied and withered into liberalism, secular humanism or neo-paganism so has the literature born of it. And so has the anti-Catholicism that was the patriotic counterpart to Protestantism.

The logical conclusion is that if we want to resist the relativism of artistic and religious values a fundamental rehabilitation of English relations with the Papacy is the only solution. We remember that at the same time as the Armada and the *Faerie Queene*, Shakespeare and his peers were inspired by Spanish tragedy, while Donne and the Caroline poets were moved by Spanish Mysticism. We remember that Carlyle described this greatest moment of English Literature as 'the outcome and flowerage of all that had preceded it... attributable to the Catholicism of the Middle Ages'.[18] And we return to Curtius, who showed how Europe has in truth one literature, mediated by the Latin Middle Ages. As we are severed from that Latin Classical tradition so we are severed from ourselves. The deluded freedom of the present is in fact a prison of the absence of a living tradition, not even the romantic Catholic or Puritan versions that counted for literary tradition after the Renaissance. This is the cultural incarnation of the doctrinal democracy of the Church of England and the relativism of post-Christian paganism.

While it is commonplace in the twenty-first century to assert that the nature of the literary enterprise has changed, the real question is whether one still exists. This may be the assertion that non-fiction has become or regained its position as literature; that it is more appropriate to the need of the society or the times that we live in. It may not even be literature in Pound's sense that 'Great literature is simply language charged with meaning to the utmost possible degree.'[19] Meaning now is simply the idea, fact or information to be communicated, rather than the artistic use of language and trope: it is, literally, prosaic. A great deal of poetry and fiction is being published, but if the dominant creative form is 'literary non-fiction', or even 'literary fiction', then whether this can be described as literature at all is questionable. With the loss of Naipaul as a creative talent, fiction in English has lost its literary power and literary non-fiction has replaced literary fiction. Ackroyd asserts that a 'revival of English literature over the last two decades has largely taken place in prose. Biographical and historical writings have flourished; what is called "literary" fiction has never held larger audiences; poetry has withered on the vine.'[20]

He also recognizes that this has occurred at the same time as a blurring of the boundaries with non-fiction. In his late fictions, *The Enigma of Arrival* (1987) and *A Way in the World* (1994), Naipaul, then, a greater writer than any other in English, experimented more and more with a mixture of autobiography, invention and history. He has written many different types of prose, fiction, history, memoir, criticism, journalism, reportage and travel writing. He has described himself as a 'manager of narrative'.[21] It is another way of saying that the novel no longer meets the requirements and demands of literature. It has ceased to be able to 'make sense of the world' as 'only nonfiction could capture the complexities of today's world'.[22] While this may be an accurate description of the English-speaking book and periodical publishing marketplace, echoed by writers and critics, such as Peter Ackroyd and V. S. Naipaul, it does not account for the demise of literature. But literature is writing as an art, not the communication of information. Despite Naipaul's experiments with autobiography and history in his novels, they are still novels, fictions, and his non-fiction is still non-fiction.

Although there are a lot of novels and poems being published today that does not mean that any of them are any good, that they have any literary merit. But it does not mean either that non-fiction prose has taken their place, even if it does include 'the great resurgence of historical writing, in the work of Jonathan Clark and Blair Worden (not to mention Eamonn Duffy)'.[23] We might also mention Maurice Cowling, Edward Norman, Patrick Wormald, and Aidan Nichols. However, whether this is a result of the literary qualities of their writing, or the quality of their ideas, of which Ackroyd approves, is important. For this is the school of historical revisionism that lies behind Ackroyd's work, which argues that English identity and religion derives from the early medieval period rather than from the Reformation. It asserts that the latter identity is an elite imposition rather than a popular movement, which only became such through identification with the patriotic cause, against the Spanish before 1688, and more generally afterwards.

This begins to look like wishful thinking, therefore, related to the fact that he practices all these disciplines himself. He also argues that 'intellectual history may soon take the place of fiction and biography as the single most important form of English prose'[24] and exemplifies this at length in *Albion*. It looks like an excuse for the fact that literature is not possible without a conception of or ground for standards, which must in the end be religious. And the withering away of poetry is a serious thing in itself. It is in part the victim of the development of the media, with recorded music, radio and television occupying the mental space required for this oral form. Prose is an art of literacy, and thus modern: but poetry is eternal, the cleansing of the tools of thought, their purification. That is why poetry is the fundamental literary art, the most spiritual, and the closest to music and to prayer.

148

In Western society the ultimate test of the civilization of a culture is its ability to perpetuate the tradition that originates in Greece and Rome. Yet while there is a lot of poetry being written and published today, perhaps more than ever before, by more people, none of it has the significance of Yeats or Eliot, or any of the great Romantic, Augustan, Stuart, Elizabethan or Medieval poets. While Eliot believed that poetry should be difficult, partly as a means of avoiding the compromises involved in writing for a wider audience, now there is very little left of any seriousness that is aimed at any audience. It is in this context that we may see the work of the poets of the post-Second World War period: Geoffrey Hill, Ted Hughes and Philip Larkin, as well as with John Betjeman, Carol Ann Duffy, Andrew Motion, C. H. Sisson, Charles Tomlinson and R. S. Thomas among others. Since Betjeman, Hughes and Larkin no poet has had as high a public profile or audience.

Larkin was an aggressive anti-modernist, who never quite rid himself of elements of their style or managed to revive the credulity of the Romantics. In his work we see the almost complete absence of Christian or classical themes, he explicitly stated that he had 'no belief in "tradition" or a common myth-kitty'.[25] And he remained the pupil of his master of melancholy and plainness, Thomas Hardy, as, in a different register, did Betjeman. English poetry is still Romantic, yet with the decline of the Protestantism that provided its spiritual context, it has lost its force. This means that even the contemporary English poets with the most 'modernist' technique, such as Ted Hughes and Geoffrey Hill, are still Romantics. It means that despite their formal modernism their metaphysics have not overcome the metaphysical problem. And it is possible that Eliot did not do so either, remaining as he did in a church without a Magisterium, still following the Book of Common Prayer, albeit in the catholicized 1928 version. When the 'conventional values' of society are those of liberal individualism, only a literary art restrained by the authority of a Magisterium or an orthodox body of doctrine and familiar with the Latin Classical tradition can be truly classical.

The central question of this study has been whether the decline in literature has been caused by the decline in Christianity. It may be argued that neither has in fact occurred, so a causal link makes no sense unless it is to argue that literature has been sustained either by the continuation of Christianity, in spite of it, or even because of it. It does not attempt to demonstrate the decline of Christianity, but it does assert that remnants, habits of mind, if they exist, are nothing without practice or observance, even if they do happen to be a practical implementation of Christian virtue. It may be argued that the rights and welfare society is an expression of the love for neighbour in Christ's teaching as indeed it is by many priests, confirming that their practical role is the sanctification of the secular state. But such ethics are in the end nothing but a protection of one's own sphere of activity or a satisfaction of one's own desires without eschatology and dogma. Although Christianity need not be practised by everyone in society for it to be Christian it must be guided by those ideas, and contemporary England is guided by secularity not belief.

Authority is the same in religion as it is in politics and in the arts. Either the individual submits to it or the ultimate authority is that of the individual. In all spheres the consequence is chaos, whether moral, social or cultural. In literature, as in the other arts, it is the chaos of the absence of tradition, the discarding of the inheritance of thousands of years. It is the insistence that the individual, the present, is sovereign. That nothing is any better than anything else except that someone says it is better for them. It is the death of literature, and it is the result of the death of religion. If we wish to reverse it, we must first attend to its causes. English anti-Catholicism has declined at the same rate as the Protestantism that was English Christianity after the Reformation. And the Papacy has been shown in recent experience to be the only body capable of resisting the 'dictatorship of relativism'.

The sole institutional basis of resistance is the authority that persists in the Roman Catholic Church in the independent doctrinal authority of the Papacy. It alone is capable of resisting the undermining of foundations that was entailed by the revision of theology to derive from the individual conscience at the Reformation, that was itself the consequence of the earlier separation of philosophy and theology. It alone can survive the 'corrosive scepticism' of modernity and offer the possibility of escape from solipsism, existentialism and nihilism. Its lesson is that authority cannot be democratic in every sphere, and that leadership may require other virtues than popularity. To some this may seem authoritarian, but to those who know it is liberation: the greatest liberation, and the founding English liberty; the liberation from sin, and with it the liberation from the earthbound life, that is, eternal life.

While many Catholics will admit that aspects of their liturgy are aesthetically inferior there is no doubt that their ability to maintain the teaching of orthodox doctrine is superior, and that, in the end, is what matters. Words and images have, at least, the potential to be divine. So they, and the arts which derive from them, are regarded, or should so be regarded, with the utmost seriousness. The loss of religious seriousness has led to an inability to use words seriously, and vice versa. The language of the Elizabethans and the Stuarts is the language of the Prayer Book and the Authorized Version: the language of literature or liturgy now is that of unbelief. While some aspects of Anglo-Catholic liturgy and its integration into English identity may in some cases be desirable, it has also become identified with apostasy and romanticism.

Reformed ideas such as Erastianism and Calvinism are developments, fragments of the idea of election, of the Chosen People. And as the other churches are splinters of the Catholic Church, of moments in its history, or fragments of its comprehensiveness, so the modern movements we have seen in literature are splinters of Latin Classical culture. We have so much to rediscover that there is a danger that it may be too much, when so much competes for our attention. The consequence is excessive cultural special-ization, the 'disintegration of the intellect'. This is where the great creative, comprehensive minds and perspectives of the arts and the Church are needed.

We have seen the history of the relationship between literature and religion in England, a history which is central to the understanding of the nature of its civilization. Who knows what, as Ackroyd might say, the 'revenants' might be. It seems likely that the modern pagan liberal situation will persist, but it is at least possible that religious absence or need will become apparent to people, and they will seek to fulfil it. As Michael Burleigh reminds us, the truth of Matthew Arnold's *Dover Beach* is that the tide of the sea of faith goes out, but it also comes back in again.[26] But the one thing we can say for sure is that it is impossible for the idea of standards and therefore of literature or any high art to persist without a religious basis or foundation. The religion of the individual conscience is Protestantism in religion, liberalism in politics, and populism in the arts. And the standards for Western literature are classical.

It may be that the 'dictatorship of relativism' in Western liberal democracies is too absolute, too complete. It may be that the only place where literature or the arts can survive is in Rome or Havana, where pagan culture is sanctified by the Papacy, not London, Paris or New York, where materialism reigns. And yet the practice of literature may itself be the very thing by which this process may be reversed: as 'the only plausible link between historic orthodoxy and any orthodoxy which is likely to command the future'.[27] Our present relativism is the consequence of the final emptying of the post-Christian morality, culture and society of the remnants of the Christian morality, culture and society that preceded it. The final stage of this process occurred after the Second World War.

In England the residual lapsed-Protestantism, the respectability and decency of the 1950s, whether accompanied by Christian practice or not, was displaced in the 1960s by a social libertarianism which was extended into the economic realm by the market reforms of the 1980s.[28] This much is the logical and natural conclusion of the previous centuries, but with it has gone the possibility of the standards which had upheld the possibility of literature or the other arts. What is suggested is that the transcendence of the romantic individualism and relativism of modern liberal art may be achieved, but only through the intellectual discipline of orthodoxy. Romantic art may be re-Classicized by the re-incarnation in it of orthodox belief. This 'inculturation' *is* possible in the condition of postmodernity and post-Anglicanism in England, as it is in traditional cultures, but only through an acceptance of the Magisterium. As Cowling concludes 'the instinct for religion which lurks beneath the indifference of the public mind, may yet surprise by its willingness to be led astray by Christianity'.[29] But that may be too much for modern people to swallow.

---

1. 'Belief was a different thing for the thirteenth, for the seventeenth, and for the nineteenth century. Donne does not "believe in" Anglican theology in the way that Dante believes in Aquinas; and Laforgue does not "believe in" Schopenhauer or Hartman in the same way as either' (Eliot, *Varieties of Metaphyscial Poetry*, p. 223).
2. Naipaul, Interview, *Financial Times* (21 August 2004). Michel Houellebecq embodies this rejection, with his relentless and unflinching, yet hopeless, portrayal of contemporary nihilism and evil. The poetry of the School of Baudelaire ended with Valéry, Eliot's contemporary, and Eliot himself.
3. Curtius, *European Literature and the Latin Middle Ages*, p. 347.
4. Martin Heidegger, 'Being and Time', *The Question concerning Technology*, p. 35.
5. E.g. John Rawls, *A Theory of Justice*. 'Rawls' account is an attempt to secure the possibility of a liberal consensus regardless of the "deep" religious or metaphysical values that the parties endorse (so long as these remain open to compromise, i.e. "reasonable")' (Wikipedia 2009 < http://en.wikipedia.org/wiki/John_Rawls>).
6. *Cowling, Religion and Public Doctrine*, vol. 2, p. xxi.

7. An English pragmatic approach was developed in which the ultimate Christian value of the family is central, remarkably given the context, by D. W. Winnicott. In it the developing relationship with the mother, in a facilitating environment provided by the father, provides the means by which the ego is lead to understand and relate to the other unselfishly. Although his public statements about religion were somewhat ambiguous, his wife asserts that he became an Anglican while at medical school. See Winnicott, *The Spontaneous Gesture*, p. xiii.

8. T. S. Eliot, 'The Function of Criticism', *Selected Prose*, p. 69; 'Tradition and the Individual Talent', *Selected Prose*, p. 38.

9. See Milbank, *Theology and Social Theory*, for the ongoing dichotomy, following Comte, between Liberalism and Positivism in modern thought and practice. Radical Orthodoxy criticizes 'post-Tridentine Catholic positivist authoritarianism' but it is quite clear that Anglicanism cannot sustain an orthodox alternative (John Milbank, *Radical Orthodoxy*, p. 2). He also maintains a Romantic literary ideal, appropriate to his non-Latin version of Catholic Christianity. See Milbank, Pickstock and Ward (eds), *Radical Orthodoxy*, Chapter 5, for 'the crankiness, the eccentricity, which frequently affects writers outside of the Latin traditions'.

10. Curtius, *European Literature and the Latin Middle Ages*, pp. 257–8.

11. Norman, *Anglican Difficulties*, p. 152.

12. Nichols, *Panther and the Hind*, p. 103.

13. Clark, *Samuel Johnson*, p. 125.

14. James Boswell, *Life of Johnson* (1763).

15. See Edward Norman, *Secularisation and Church and Society in England*, 1770–1970, for the history of the English clergy's reflection of the views of their class.

16. Disraeli's answer was, 'My Lord, I am on the side of the angels. I repudiate with indignation and abhorrence these new-fangled theories' (Benjamin Disraeli, Earl of Beaconsfield, speech at Oxford Diocesan Conference, 25 November 1864).

17. Ackroyd, *Albion*, p. 128.

18. Carlyle, 'Hero as Poet'.

19. Pound, *ABC of Reading*, p. 28.

20. *The Times* (2 January 2002).

21. Naipaul, *Beyond Belief*, Prologue. He elsewhere describes the preference for the novel over other forms of prose as a 'Bloomsbury prejudice'.

22. Rachael Donadio, interview with V. S. Naipaul, *New York Times* (7 August 2005).

23. Peter Ackroyd, *The Times* (2 January 2002).

24. Peter Ackroyd, *The Times* (27 October 1994), in a review of Clark, *Samuel Johnson*.

25. He continued, 'To me the whole of the ancient world, the whole of

classical and biblical mythology means very little, and I think that using them today not only fills poems full of dead spots, but dodges the writer's duty to be original.'

26. Burleigh, *Earthly Powers*, p. 252.

27. Cowling, *Religion and Public Doctrine*, vol. 3, p. 698.

28. 'It is interesting to note that the "sexual revolution" is usually portrayed as a communist utopia, whereas in fact it was simply another stage in the rise of the individual... The sexual revolution was to destroy the last unit ["the couple and the family"] separating the individual from the market' (Michel Houellebecq, *Atomised*, pp. 135–6). Something similar may have happened in America: see Joseph Bottum, 'The Death of Protestant America'.

29. Cowling, *Religion and Public Doctrine*, vol. 3, p. 701.

Bibliography

Ackroyd, Peter, *Albion: The Origins of the English Imagination* (London: Vintage, 2002).

Ackroyd, Peter, *T. S. Eliot: A Life* (London: Penguin, 1994).

Baldick, Chris, *Criticism and Literary Theory 1890 to the Present* (London: Longman, 1996).

Baudelaire, Charles-Pierre, *Selected Writings on Art and Literature*, trans P. Charvet (Harmondsworth: Penguin, 1992).

Benedict XVI, *Faith, Reason and the University – Memories and Reflections* (Regensburg: University of Regensburg, Tuesday, 12 September 2006) <www.vatican.va/holy_father/benedict_xvi/speeches/2006/september/documents/hf_ben-xvi_spe_20060912_university-regensburg_en.html>. *See also* Ratzinger, Joseph.

Benítez-Rojo, Antonio, *The Repeating Island: The Caribbean and the Postmodern Perspective*, trans. James E. Maraniss (Durham, CA, and London: Duke University Press, 1992).

Blond, Philip (ed.), *Post-secular Philosophy: Between Philosophy and Theology* (London: Routledge, 1997).

Bloom, Harold, *The American Religion* (New York: Simon and Schuster, 1992).

Booker, Christopher, *The Seven Basic Plots* (London: Continuum, 2004).

Boswell, James, *Life of Johnson* (1763); edited, from the two-volume Oxford edition of 1904, by Jack Lynch <http://andromeda.rutgers.edu/~jlynch/Texts/BLJ/blj63.html>.

Bottum, Joseph, 'The Death of Protestant America: A Political Theory of the Protestant Mainline', *First Things* (August/September 2008), pp. 23–33.

Bottum, Joseph, 'What T. S. Eliot Almost Believed', *First Things* (August/September 1995), pp. 25–30.

Brewer, Derek, 'Medieval European Literature', in Boris Ford (ed.), *Medieval Literature: The European Inheritance*, New Pelican Guide to English Literature, vol. 1, part 2 (London: Penguin, 1984), pp. 41–81.

Burleigh, Michael, *Earthly Powers: Relgion and Politics in Europe from the Enlightenment to the Great War* (London: HarperCollins, 2005).

Carpenter, Humphrey, *A Serious Character: The Life of Ezra Pound* (Boston: Houghton Mifflin, 1988).

Clark, J. C. D., *Samuel Johnson: Literature, Religion and English Cultural Politics from the Restoration to Romanticism* (Cambridge: Cambridge University Press, 1994).

Clark, J. C. D., *Our Shadowed Present: Modernism, Postmodernism and History* (London: Atlantic, 2003).

Cowling, Maurice, *Religion and Public Doctrine in Modern England*, 3 vols (Cambridge: Cambridge University Press, 1980, 1985, 2001).

Curtius, Ernst R., *European Literature and the Latin Middle Ages*, trans. Willard R. Trask (Princeton, NJ: Princeton University Press, 1990).

Dante Alighieri, *Paradiso*, trans. John D. Sinclair (Oxford: Oxford University Press, 1939).

Davie, Donald, *With the Grain: Essays on Thomas Hardy and Modern British Poetry* (Manchester: Carcanet, 1998).

Duffy, Eamon, *The Stripping of the Altars: Traditional Religion in England*, 1400–1580 (New Haven: Yale University Press, 1992).

Eliot, T. S., *After Strange Gods: A Primer of Modern Heresy* (London: Faber and Faber, 1934).

Eliot, T. S., 'Little Gidding' (1942), *The Complete Poems and Plays of T. S. Eliot* (London: Faber and Faber, 1969).

Eliot, T. S., *Notes towards the Definition of Culture* (London: Faber and Faber, 1962).

Eliot, T. S., 'Religion without Humanism', in Norman Foerster, ed., *Humanism and America* (New York: Farrar and Rinehart, 1930), pp. 105–11.

Eliot, T. S., *The Sacred Wood: Essays on Poetry and Criticism* (London: Methuen, 1920).

Eliot, T. S., *Selected Prose*, ed. Frank Kermode (London: Faber and Faber, 1975).

Eliot, T. S., *The Varieties of Metaphysical Poetry*, ed. Ronald Schuchard (Orlando: Harcourt Brace, 1994).

Funkenstein, Amos, *Theology and the Scientific Imagination: From the Middle Ages to the Seventeenth Century* (Princeton, NJ; Guildford: Princeton University Press, 1986).

Godman, Peter, 'Epilogue', in Curtius, *European Literature and the Latin Middle Ages*, pp. 599–653.

Graham-Dixon, Andrew, *A History of British Art* (London: BBC, 1996).

Gray, John, *Straw Dogs: Thoughts on Humans and Other Animals* (London: Granta, 2003).

Gutiérrez, Pedro Juan, *The Insatiable Spiderman* (London: Faber and Faber, 2005).

Heidegger, Martin, 'Being and Time' (1927), *The Question concerning Technology and Other Essays*, trans. William Lovitt (New York: Harper, 1977).

Hopkins, Gerard Manley, *Poems and Prose*, ed. W. H. Gardner (London: Penguin Classics, 1985).

Hopper, Kenneth, and William Hopper, *The Puritan Gift* (London: I. B. Tauris, 2007).

Houellebecq, Michel, *Atomised*, trans. Frank Wynne (*Les Particules élémentaires* [1998]; London: Heinemann, 2001).

Hughes, Ted, *Shakespeare and the Goddess of Complete Being* (London: Faber and Faber, 1992).

Hughes, Ted, *Winter Pollen* (New York: Picador, 1995).

Humphreys, Arthur, 'The Social Setting', in Boris Ford (ed.), *From Dryden to Johnson*, New Pelican Guide to English Literature, vol. 3 (London: Penguin, 1991), pp. 15–50.

John Paul II , Address to Afro-Americans Santo Domingo (12 October 1992).

John Paul II, *Memory and Identity: Personal Reflections* (London: Weidenfeld & Nicolson, 2005).

Johnson, Samuel, *The Lives of the Most Eminent English Poets, With Critical Observations on their Works*, vol. 1 'The Life Of Cowley' (1779), <http://andromeda.rutgers.edu/~jlynch/Texts/cowley.html>.

Larkin, Philip, *Required Writing* (London: Faber and Faber, 1983).

Leo XIII, *Testem Benovolentiae Nostrae* (1899) <http://www.ewtn.com/library/PAPALDOC/L13TESTE.HTM>.

Leonard, Graham, 'Preface', in Aidan Nichols, *The Panther and the Hind*, pp. xi–xii.

Milbank, John, *Theology and Social Theory: Beyond Secular Reason* (2nd edn; Oxford: Blackwell, 2006).

Milbank, John, Catherine Pickstock and Graham Ward (eds), *Radical Orthodoxy* (London: Routledge, 1999).

Monk, Ray, *How to Read Wittgenstein* (London: Granta, 2005).

Naipaul, V. S., *Among the Believers* (London: Picador, 2001).

Naipaul, V. S., *Beyond Belief: Islamic Excursions among the Converted Peoples* (London: Abacus, 1999).

Naipaul, V. S., *The Enigma of Arrival* (Harmondsworth: Penguin, 1988).

Naipaul, V. S., *Literary Occasions: Essays*, introd. and ed. Pankaj Mishra (London: Picador, 2003).

Naipaul, V. S., 'Our Universal Civilization', lecture to the Manhattan Institute (30 October 1990).

Naipaul, V. S., *The Return of Eva Peron* (Harmondsworth: Penguin, 1981).

Nichols, Aidan, *Christendom Awake* (Edinburgh: T&T Clark, 1999).

Nichols, Aidan, *The Panther and the Hind* (Edinburgh: T&T Clark, 1994).

Nichols, Aidan, 'A Personal View of Anglican Uniatism', Address to Anglican Use Society, on their and Forward in Faith website, abridged version in *New Directions* (Summer 2005) <www.anglicanuse.org/Anglican_Uniatism.pdf>.

Nichols, Aidan, *The Thought of Benedict XVI: An Introduction to the Theology of Joseph Ratzinger* (London: Burns & Oates, 2005).

Norman, Edward, *Anglican Difficulties* (London: Continuum, 2004).

Norman, Edward, *Church and Society in England, 1770–1970: A Historical Study* (Oxford: Clarendon Press, 1976).

Norman, Edward, *Secularisation* (London: Continuum, 2002).

Norman, Edward, *The Roman Catholic Church: An Illustrated History* (Berkeley, CA: University of California Press, 2007).

Norman, *Edward, Roman Catholicism in England from the Elizabethan Settlement to the Second Vatican Council* (Oxford: Oxford University Press, 1985).

Oddie, William, *The Roman Option* (London: Harper Collins, 1997).

Orwell, George, *The Collected Essays, Journalism and Letters of George Orwell*, ed. Sonia Orwell and Ian Angus (London: Secker & Warburg. 1968).

Pickstock, Catherine, *After Writing: On the Liturgical Consummation of Philosophy*, Challenges in Contemporary Theology (Oxford: Blackwell, 1998).

Plato, *The Dialogues of Plato*, trans. Benjamin Jowett, 4 vols (Oxford: Clarendon Press, 1871).

Pound, Ezra, *The ABC of Reading* (London: Faber and Faber, 1991).

Powell-Ward, John, *The English Line: Poetry of the Unpoetic from Wordsworth to Larkin* (London: Macmillan, 1991).

Ratzinger, Joseph, 'Homily at the Mass for the Election of the Roman Pontiff' (18 April 2005).

Ratzinger, Joseph, *Introduction to Christianity* (San Francisco: Ignatius Press, 1990).

Ratzinger, Joseph, *The Nature and Mission of Theology* (San Francisco: Ignatius Press, 1995). See also Benedict XVI.

Rawls, John, *A Theory of Justice* (Oxford: Oxford University Press, 1999).

Robinson, Ian, 'Prose and Dissociation', in Boris Ford (ed.), *From Donne to Marvell*, New Pelican Guide to English Literature, vol. 3 (London: Penguin), pp. 260–72.

Schama, Simon, *A History of Britain: At the Edge of the World? 3000 BC – AD 1603*, vol. 1 (London: BBC Books, 2000).

Scruton, Roger, *An Intelligent Person's Guide to Modern Culture* (London: Duckworth, 1998)

Scruton, Roger, *A Short History of Modern Philosophy: From Descartes to Wittgenstein* (London: Routledge, 1995).

Sisson, C. H., *The Avoidance of Literature: Collected Essays [of] C. H. Sisson*, ed. Michael Schmidt (Manchester: Carcanet New Press, 1978).

Steiner, George, *Real Presences: Is There Anything in What We Say?* (London: Faber, 1989).

Stern, Bernard Herbert, *The Rise of Romantic Hellenism in English Literature 1732–1786* (Menasha: G. Banta, 1940).

Taylor, Dennis, *Hardy's Metres and Victorian Prosody: With a Metrical Appendix of Hardy's Stanza Forms* (Oxford: Clarendon Press, 1988).

Voegelin, Eric, *The Political Religions (Die politischen Religionen*, 1938), The Collected Works of Eric Voegelin, Volume 5, *Modernity without Restraint*, ed. with an Introduction by Manfred Henningsen (Columbia, MO: University of Missouri Press, 1999).

Winnicott, Donald Woods, *The Spontaneous Gesture: Selected Letters of D. W. Winnicott*, ed. F. Robert Rodman (Cambridge, MA; London: Harvard University Press, 1987).

Wormald, Patrick, 'Anglo-Saxon Society and Its Literature', in M. R. Godden and M. Lapidge (eds), *Cambridge Companion to Old English Literature* (Cambridge: Cambridge University Press, 1992), pp. 1–19.

Wormald, Patrick, 'Bede, "Beowulf" and the Conversion of the Anglo-Saxon Aristocracy', in R. T. Farrell (ed.), *Bede and Anglo-Saxon England* (Oxford: British Archaeological Reports, 1978), pp. 32–95.

Wormald, Patrick, 'Bede, the *Bretwaldas* and the Origins of the *gens Anglorum*', in P. Wormald, Donald Bullough and Roger Collins (eds), *Ideal and Reality in Frankish and Anglo-Saxon Society: Studies Presented to J. M. Wallace-Hadrill* (Oxford: Blackwell, 1983), pp. 99–129.

Wormald, Patrick, 'Enga Lond: The Making of an Allegiance', *Journal of Historical Sociology* 7:1 (March 1994), pp. 1–24.